Antonio C. N. Gallenga

Italy

present and future - Vol. 2

Antonio C. N. Gallenga

Italy
present and future - Vol. 2

ISBN/EAN: 9783337230616

Printed in Europe, USA, Canada, Australia, Japan

Cover: Foto ©Andreas Hilbeck / pixelio.de

More available books at **www.hansebooks.com**

ITALY, PRESENT AND FUTURE

BY

A. GALLENGA

AUTHOR OF

"SOUTH AMERICA," "RUSSIA," "THE PEARL OF THE ANTILLES,"
ETC., ETC.

IN TWO VOLUMES

VOL. II.

LONDON: CHAPMAN AND HALL
LIMITED

1887

CONTENTS OF VOL. II.

I. Schools.

II. High Schools.

III. Poetry and the Drama.

IV. Romance and History.

IX.   Conclusion.

ITALY, PRESENT AND FUTURE.

CHAPTER I.

SCHOOLS.

The Church as an Instructress—Condition of Popular Instruction in Italy at the Reconstruction of the Kingdom—Efforts of the Italian Government to improve it—Difficulties it had to contend with—Instruction *v.* Education—Godly and Godless Schools—Superior Instruction—Universities—Their Number—Their Efficiency—Other Institutions—Their Purpose.

BETWEEN the Church and the School, from the earliest stages of society, there has been at all times close intimacy. For a very long time learning was the priest's monopoly, and when he condescended to impart the mere rudiments of knowledge to a few laymen, he took his stand on the principle that "the fear of the Lord" was to be not merely "the beginning," but also the end "of wisdom," and approved of no other instruction than what emanated from the sanctuary. Both Alfred's and Charlemagne's primitive scholastic establishments were purely monastic,

and ten centuries of reforms and revolutions have
hardly as yet wholly obliterated from Oxford or Paris
the claustral character which those schools received
from their founders.

In Roman Catholic as well as in Protestant communities, the priest, when he was no longer the
teacher, insisted at least on being the controller of
all teachers.   Colleges and universities were never
without the guidance of some clerical rector or chancellor, inspector or proctor; and it was for such to
prescribe both the quantity and quality of the intellectual food on which the learner was to be
nourished.

It was not long, however, before the connection
between Church and School resolved itself into antagonism.   The lay mind hungered after what its
religious instructor withheld as the forbidden fruit
of the tree of knowledge of good and evil.   No free
school could be opened without being denounced as
" Godless."   And in the school that was called
" Godly " the teacher virtually used the two-horned
argument attributed to Mahomet's disciples, arguing
that " either the doctrine taught in any other school
than his own was true, and it could only be what
the Church taught, or it was something else than

what the Church taught, and then it must necessarily be false, damnable doctrine."

From the first establishment of the Jesuits as general directors of educational institutions, there was in Italy, for the students of all upper and middle classes, an end of all freedom of learning. But for the great mass of the lower orders there was absolutely an end of all learning. For a few scores of the people's children in the cities, the establishments of the monks of the *Scuole Pie*, or *Scolopii*, and those of the *Ignorantelli*, or *Ignorantins* (the latter a French importation), served as grammar schools of the most primitive description. But as to the whole mass of the rural population, it was suffered to lie in utter darkness. For the priest, like a very dog in the manger, after carrying on a victorious war against all other schools, ended by closing his own, all his Sunday instruction in the parish church being limited to the catechism learnt by heart without book, and prayers in an unknown tongue.

The result of three centuries of this system of *obscurantism* was made manifest by the difficulties the Italian Government had to contend with in their endeavours to break through it. Upon the first census of the emancipated country being taken, in

1861, it appeared that out of 18,817,643 persons of
more than ten years of age, 14,053,502 (*i. e.* 74
per cent of the population) could neither read nor
write. Twenty years later, 1881, the proportion of
analfabeti, or utterly illiterate, had been reduced to
62 per cent, a notable progress. But in this, as in
every other branch of social development, the difference between the various regions of the country was
strikingly apparent ; for the percentage of the un-
lettered, excluding children, in Upper Italy (Piedmont,
Liguria, Lombardy, Venetia) was only 48·85 ; in
Central Italy, 64·61 ; in Southern Italy, 79·46 ; and
in the islands (Sicily and Sardinia), 80·91. Ignorance
thus proceeded from north to south, till we find, at
the two extremities of the scale, the province of
Turin with 25·10 per cent (the *Zenith*), and that of
Cosenza in Calabria with 86·35 (the *Nadir*) of
scholastic learning.

The Italian Government was greatly alarmed by
a state of things which they deemed incompatible
with the free institutions with which the country
had been so suddenly trusted ; they took for granted,
perhaps somewhat too hastily, that a people's morality
must needs be on a par with their intellectual acquirements, and resolved that, whether or not their

lower classes might be *educated*, they should at all
events be *instructed*. The following facts will give
us some idea of the nature of that instruction.

The various laws promulgated from 1859 to 1883
prescribed the foundation of elementary schools, male
and female, in all the 8258 communes of the Italian
kingdom, compelling the parents under a pecuniary
penalty to send their children to school, and this
enactment was complied with in 8116 communes.
In all the other communes (*i. e.* in 142) there was
not a sufficient number of schools, though there was
one school at least in every commune.

In 1883 these schools (day schools) in the kingdom
of Italy were 42,390, frequented by 1,873,713 pupils,
of whom 1,017,402 were boys, and 856,311 girls.
Adding to these all other schools, *i. e.* private
elementary schools, night schools, Sunday schools,
gymnasiums, lyceums, universities, and other teaching
institutions of all kind and quality, we shall find
that 2,576,072 persons (about ten per cent of the
population more than six years old, which amounted
to 24,800,000) received in that year some kind of
instruction.

Popular instruction in Italy was to be universal,
compulsory, and gratuitous; and the schools were

equally to be open to pupils of all denominations. But besides the public or Government schools there were also private elementary schools, many of them under priestly direction; and by frequenting these latter, children were, under certain conditions, exempted from the duty of attending the former. The private elementary schools in Italy, in 1883, were 7129, with 163,099 pupils—57,437 boys, and 105,662 girls. While the males in the public schools considerably outnumbered the females, in the private schools there were nearly two females to one male.

At the bottom of this difference there obviously lies the religious question.

When, in the hope of settling that question, Count Cavour put forth that famous phrase, "A free Church in a free State," he did not perhaps sufficiently consider on what principle his formula should or could be applied to public instruction. If the State was to be neutral in all matters appertaining to religion, it seems evident that there could be no religious instruction imparted in the Government or national schools. If the State was "*Godless*," Godless must also be all State education. Children should learn reading and writing in the lay schools, and they should go for their catechism to their parish church, or to the chapel, synagogue, or "*temple*," as every dissenting Christian Church is somewhat contemptuously called in Italy, being thus stigmatized as something heathenish.

The problem seemed thus easily solved in theory; practically, however, it was fraught with grave, almost insurmountable difficulties.

The State might care very little about the people's religion, but it could not be equally indifferent about their morality ; and although it might be taken for granted that sound morals lie at the bottom of all religious instruction, still, having established the principle of religious freedom and equality, it could not compel attendance at clerical schools by the same right that empowered it to enforce it at its own public and lay schools. The State could not insist on all children learning the catechism, though it made it imperative on them to master the *a, b, c*.

It is perfectly true that, while the law allowed every man the free choice of a religion, it did not in plain words admit of an open profession of irreligion. And it is also unquestionable that for the immense majority of the Italians the alternative lies between Roman Catholicism and no religion at all. Still, in sober fact, the option in this matter is tacitly left to

every man, and the number of those who, openly or
in their hearts, avail themselves of this freedom is
large beyond conception. Rampant or blatant in-
fidelity is indeed not very common, but infinite
doubt and unreasoning denial are everywhere prevalent; and stronger than either is utter contempt
of the priest, and of the many "gross superstitions"
on which, his adversaries contend, his ascendancy
over the defenceless masses is based.

To reconcile all opinions, although elementary
instruction was made obligatory, it was equally
obtainable in public or private schools; and the
greatest number of these latter were clerical; and
whatever religious instruction was there imparted
was in no manner interfered with, the State only
troubling itself about the proficiency of the pupils
in their ordinary lay studies. This arrangement,
however, failed to give satisfaction to either of the
contending parties. For the clericals complained
that "although Government tolerated private schools,
it did not endow them as it did its own schools; and
although it gave them nothing, it reserved the right
of inspecting them, and of assuring itself of the
capacity of their teachers and of the proficiency of
their pupils, just as if it defrayed their expenses."

Still the gravest and strongest grievance of the clericals was, that "what Government considered fair neutrality, was to them in fact bitter hostility; that every teacher in the Government schools was an open apostle of atheism and immorality; that any good influence they, the priestly instructors, might exercise over the small flock of their own pupils, was counteracted by the pernicious doctrines sown broadcast among the vast multitude in the lay schools; that they, the priests, came into the lists enormously weighted, and with fearful odds against them; and that the poison of impious maxims was thus spread in juvenile minds which neither the teaching in the Sunday schools, nor any amount of preaching later in life, could have power to root out. The private schools were merely a grain of salt unable to preserve society from the mass of foul corruption engendered by the baneful influence of the public schools."

On the other hand, the anti-clerical, or, as it is called, "Liberal" party, referred to the evidence of the past to prove "that the tendency of all priestly teaching was to dwarf, to unnerve, and degrade the children's intellect, by giving undue preponderance to the master's *word* over the pupil's *sense;* that the

priest's only means of imposing belief was proscrip-
tion of the use of reason ; that with the intent of
sanctifying his disciples, he merely unmanned them ;
that with Jesuitism at its head, a nation was only
taught to indulge in subtlety and casuistry, in quibble
and chicanery, till the very instinct of plain, sober,
fearless truth is stifled in its heart.

" Certainly," they insist, " as long as the priest
was the only schoolmaster, the complete intellectua
darkness to which the lower classes were doomed
was no preservative against their moral depravation.
Indeed it may be asserted," they argued, " that, far
from deterring, it rather encouraged and perpetuated
crime. Witness the little images and scapularies worn
by Roman and Neapolitan brigands next to the skin,
in homage to some Madonna or patron saint, relying
upon them as amulets or talismans, not only to
insure beforehand forgiveness of the deeds of outrage
and bloodshed upon which they were bent, but also
to implore heavenly aid to guarantee them from the
carabineer's bullets. Witness the shocking case very
lately reported in a Paris trial, of a French adulteress
(a woman not of the lowest ranks), who, while her
paramour was at work ridding her of her husband
by assassination, was kneeling at the Virgin's altar in

the nearest church, offering up prayers and alms to obtain from the Queen of Heaven a 'happy fulfilment of her secret, *i. e.* murderous, intentions.'"

It is especially on the education of women that the priests in Italy strive to maintain their hold; and that explains the fact of the female pupils in private schools so greatly outnumbering the males. Strange enough! In this respect the priests are countenanced not merely by the mass of their most bigoted devotees, but even by the most advanced Liberals and profound freethinkers. For an Italian is apt to think that what is good for himself and his boys may be bad for his wife and daughters; that although a little scepticism or agnosticism may become a man of spirit and with some pretension to ability to judge for himself, passive, submissive religion is and must always be the greatest ornament of woman, the fittest and most proper safeguard of all feminine purity. And, with these views, the same father who would almost kill his sons rather than trust them to those " mere hot-beds of Jesuitism, the *Scolopian* and *Ignorantin* brotherhood," is only too glad to place his girls under the tuition of the pure and holy but not less narrow-minded and superstitious Ursuline sisterhoods. The notion that " women may still have a soul to save," though men care not for their own, is not yet completely rooted out of the Italian masculine mind.

This blind mutual intolerance, this implacable antagonism between clericals and Liberals, is not limited to the teachers of elementary schools, but equally runs through every description of superior educational institutions, arraying the whole youth of the country in hostile ranks, and making of the Italian nation a house divided against itself. In 1884 the public gymnasiums, national or municipal, were 322, with 25,570 students; the private gymnasiums 156, with 6996 students; the public lyceums were 135, with 9994 students; the private ones 65, and their students 2015. By far the greatest number of all these private establishments were in the priests' hands. Besides these there were also, in the same year, 245 gymnasiums with 12,554 students connected with the bishops' seminaries, and 141 episcopal lyceums with 2666 students. The same proportions were observable in all branches of superior instruction, till we reached the universities, from which the theological faculty has been, or is being, banished, its proper place being assigned to it in the episcopal seminaries.

In some of the private lyceums and gymnasiums,

it must be allowed, the instruction is, to say the least, at par with that imparted in the public institutions; but the choice of the parents is hardly ever influenced by considerations of the teacher's ability or character. It is the shibboleth of the "Godly" or "Godless" that settles the question; and this will hardly cause us in England much surprise, if we are told that the rector of one of the most flourishing *Godly* institutions in a provincial city of Central Italy, himself a very pious man, complained that both himself and his pupils were under the thumb of a priestly inspector who had banished from their library such a well-known, harmless, and strictly moral and religious book as Niccolini's 'Arnaldo da Brescia,' because, forsooth, it was put down in the *Index*, ages ago, as inimical to the Pope's temporal power.

We all know how sadly these religious animosities stand in the way of educational progress in all European communities; how, even in England, "of board-schools" your Roman Catholics, as well as many Dissenters, "will have none," insisting that "exclusively secular education is the greatest of moral evils," and protesting against a tax which "as yet has been productive of nothing but mischief." But

in England, as in all other countries, the question is
simply moral and religious. In Italy alone the question
is political, national, vital. So long as an infallible
Pope denounces, *ex cathedra*, the Italian Government
as a "sacrilegious spoiler," so long as he claims an
earthly sovereignty which must be rebuilt on the
disruption and ruin of the country, there will be no
room for Niccolini, or indeed for Dante, in priestly
colleges; there will be no end to that mistrust between the Pope's priests and the King's subjects
which precludes all possibility of their co-operation
in any good undertaking, and, least of all, in the
intellectual and moral development of the rising
generation.

This state of latent or open warfare between Church
and State, if carried on to any great length, can
certainly bode no good to the Church; but neither
can it fail to embarrass and injure the State, as,
apart from all religious considerations and purely on
economical grounds, there can be no doubt that in
matter of popular education, the clergy, if friendly,
would be the most powerful and useful auxiliary to
the laity. In a country like Italy, where instruction
has so long been neglected, the dearth of able and
decent persons willing to take upon themselves the

task of schoolmasters, with such paltry remuneration as the State can afford, is very grievously felt, and the 124 Normal schools with 9416 pupils (69 of them, with 596 students, Government schools) intended to fill up the void, will hardly give satisfactory results, so long as a man of any education, and with a brave spirit in him, has a chance of a better paid and more looked up to employment than the teaching trade. Bills have been repeatedly, and even very lately, brought into the Italian Chambers for improving the condition of all Government officials, and especially for a general rise of the schoolmasters' salaries ; but it is not only money, and the little money that Italy can spare, that will raise the self-respect and importance of the mere elementary instructor.

Now there are in Italy thousands of needy mass-priests and unfrocked monks whose services might be utilized in the primary schools, and especially in those communes in which the laws on Popular Instruction are still to a great extent a dead letter, and there seems to be no reason why the Government should not come to terms with the most available of them. A priest debarred from marriage, and having, besides, his Mass and other Church services with their perquisites to depend upon, or a monk with

500 lire (£20) a year allowed as an indemnity on the suppression of his order, would, at the head of a village school, find himself in a far better condition than that of a lay teacher, with no other income than his meagre school salary, especially if burdened, as it happens in too many cases, with a wife and a numerous family.

Such a compromise, however, is not to be thought of so long as low class priests and monks, backed by an ignorant peasantry, constitute the rank and file of the main army on which the Pope, profiting by the chapter of accidents, still seems to rely for the recovery of his place among reigning potentates.

The men at present at the head of the Italian Government, although they sprang from the Radical ranks, did not wish, or did not dare, to put the strictest interpretation on their own educational law. For instance, with respect to the cross hanging on the wall of the school-room, they declared themselves neutral, referring the question to the local authorities, who in this matter, as in that of out-door processions and other Church shows, are left to act upon their own discretion and responsibility.

Undoubtedly, in everything concerning the enlightenment of the people, Italian rulers acted with too great a zeal and haste, with a faith and consistency worthy of a better cause. They were too sure of the good results a mere initiation into the mysteries of the three R's might be expected to have on the moral regeneration of the popular character. They did not consider that the tree of knowledge bears enough evil fruit at least to counteract all the good that may be expected of it. In a country going through a period of transition, where the law has undeniably lost not a little of the curb it should put on men's worst propensities, the sudden and total removal of religious guidance in the training of youthful minds must undoubtedly be fraught with serious danger. On the other hand, there is no nation that would now put up with such religious guidance as three centuries of misrule had forced upon the people of Italy. It is for the Italian Church to see whether she can so modify her religious instruction as to fit it for the exigencies of a free people. It is for the Italian Government to consider whether it can establish the freedom of its schools on such grounds as may admit of sound moral and religious guidance and control. It is, above all things, for the Pope to decide whether he harbours towards his countrymen that same paternal heart which he seems to have for other nations, and especially for those independent of his spiritual supremacy, such as England and Germany, Russia and China. With the Turk himself his Holiness deals with greater benevolence than with Italy.

In the mean while, to diffuse such good or evil as the mere rudiments of learning may work among the present generation, the Italian Government, not satisfied with its 10,528 evening schools for the adult, attended by 398,467 persons, have enacted that every man in the ranks of the national army and navy should be taught reading, writing, etc., in barracks or on board ship, throughout the time of his service; such time being prolonged by an additional year in all cases in which the required proficiency in that elementary knowledge has not been attained. And as both the service itself and attendance at school are equally obligatory on all Italian subjects, it follows that many years will not elapse before such a blessing as purely lay education may be called, is extended over the whole population of the kingdom.

As to the branches of higher instruction for the upper and middle classes, ample provision had already been made in Italy in the worst of times, the only innovation introduced into them being their emancipation from ecclesiastical thraldom.

Italy can still boast her twenty-one universities, with 13,576 students ; and they are the same as rose at different periods, owing to the former divisions of the country, either in the free cities or in the petty States where the princes emulated the munificence of great sovereigns. There is no doubt that these institutions are vastly in excess of the wants of the population, and, moreover, not so distributed as to suit the convenience of the largest numbers. In the north, seven of them—Turin, Pavia, Padua, Parma, Modena, Bologna, and Ferrara—are clustered together in the valley of the Po at the distance of 45 to 120 kilometres from one another by rail, with a population of eleven and a half millions ; while in the south, Naples alone is deemed sufficient for all the provinces of the mainland, with a population of seven and a half millions. There are, besides, one in Genoa, two for Tuscany, four for the Marches and Umbria, and one in Rome. Again, in the islands, Sicily, with a population of less than three millions of people, has three universities, Palermo, Messina, Catania ; and Sardinia requires two, Cagliari and Sassari, for only 680,000 inhabitants.

With respect to the efficiency of these institutions, it needs only be observed that, while the aggregate of them in 1884 mustered 1925 teachers, *i. e.* professors, ordinary, and extraordinary, and temporary substitutes (*Incaricati*), with 13,333 students, only two of them could, as to numbers, rank with some of the great establishments of the same description in Transalpine countries; and these two were Turin, with 2110 students, and Naples, with 3680; the tendency in our age being to forsake the quiet and forlorn cities, such as Padua, Pavia, and Pisa, the ancient seats of learning, giving preference to the larger centres of social life, in consideration of the ampler means these latter supply for the requirements of modern sciences, and of the greater convenience of their eminent cultivators. In Rome, now the capital, the university, a recent creation, built on the ruins of the late Papal *Sapenza* (hitherto with doubtful success), numbered, in 1884, 1101 students and 82 teachers. In Bologna, the ancient *Mater Studiorum*, the students, in the same year, were 1019; at Padua the students were 978; at Pavia, 872; at Pisa, 612; at Genoa, 720; at Palermo, 764. Parma, Modena, Siena, Messina, Catania, Cagliari boasted about 200 students each; while Ferrara, Macerata, Perugia,

Urbino, Camerino, and Sassari barely reached 100. In Sassari, for instance, in 1884, the students were only 102, with 26 teachers, and at Ferrara, 18 teachers for 29 students : that is, more than one master to two pupils.

More than two-thirds of these superannuated high schools are merely parasite encumbrances; but all attempts to rid the country of them have foundered against the old municipal spirit—the same spirit which in some measure contributed to oppose the reduction of the two hundred and fifty-four Italian dioceses, every town, however insignificant, clinging to such vain distinction and such meagre substantial advantages as the rank of an episcopal and university city may confer upon it. Four of the universities, Ferrara, Perugia, Camerino, and Urbino, have been declared "*free*," and these subsist, either on endowments of their own, or on subventions of their respective towns and provinces. All the others are " State Universities," more or less supported at the expense of the Government.

Besides all these, however, there are other institutions (*Istituti di Perfezionamento*, or *Di Studi Superiori*), properly speaking upper universities or finishing schools, in Milan, Florence, and other large cities, to say nothing of upper special schools, normal schools, and higher institutions, of which it would be needless to give here a minute enumeration.[1]

The aim of Italian rulers seems to have been to favour that universal upward movement from class to class, which, under the designation of "*La Carrière ouverte aux talents*," was looked upon by the revolutionists of Republican and Imperial France as the ideal of a thoroughly civilized society. They wished to *popularize*, to *democratize* the highest as well as the lowest branches of instruction; to supply the whole rising generation with the amplest, cheapest, ubiquitous means of fitting themselves for any station

---

[1] The most conspicuous are the *Istituto di Studi Superiori e di Perfezionamento* (Upper Finishing Institute) at Florence, the *Scuole di applicazione per gl' Ingegneri* (practical schools for Civil Engineers), at Rome, in Turin, Bologna, and Naples; the *Scuole Superiori di Medicina Veterinaria* (Upper Veterinary Schools), in Milan, Turin, and Naples; *Istituti Superiori di Magistero Femminile* (Upper Ladies' Colleges), at Rome and Florence; *Scuole Superiori d'Agricoltura* (Upper Agricultural Schools), in Milan and Portici; a School of Social Sciences at Florence, a Scientific and Literary Academy at Milan, an Industrial Museum at Turin, and Upper Normal Schools at Milan and Pisa, an Upper Naval School in Genoa, an Upper Commercial School in Venice, an Upper School for Sulphur Mines at Palermo, a Forestal Institute at Vallombrosa, etc., etc., all superior institutions, upon which of course minor establishments depend, and of which one, at the utmost, ought to be sufficient for the whole kingdom.

within the scope and to the full bent of their aspirations.

The intent was good and laudable. But what the results of this endless multiplication of every imaginable nursery of learning may be, in the first place in the advancement of knowledge itself, then in the furtherance of the economical and financial as well as of the social and moral interests of a nation, is a matter on which there may be more than one opinion —a matter on which I shall reserve my own for full development in another chapter.

CHAPTER II.

HIGH SCHOOLS.

Mental Gifts of the Italians—Past Energy and Present Infirmity of Purpose—Working for Bread and working for Work's sake—Influence of Climate—Want of proper Stimulus—Effects of Training—Character of Italian Universities—Want of Self-Guidance—Of Upward Aspirations—Professional and Utilitarian Instincts—Want of Bread and Thirst for Knowledge.

In spite of all the envy and hatred, malice and uncharitableness, which for thousands of years pursued the children of Israel, was there ever one individual of that scattered race whom their worst enemy could single out and say, "There goes a stupid Jew"?

And as to the Jews, to the Greeks, and other privileged nations, so to the Italians also the gift of rather more than average intellectual powers has been seldom denied. In all branches of science, literature, and art the Italians held for a long time indisputably, and by the admission of all rivals, the first rank. And this justice was done by their neighbours to the Italians of the Christian era, rather than to their progenitors, the conquerors of the world. For letters, arts, and sciences in ancient Rome were mere exotics, the luxuriancy of which choked up and rooted out all plants of indigenous growth, and left no ground for the development of new spontaneous production. So long as Greece lived, Roman Italy had hardly any intellectual existence of her own. But to the mediæval and modern Italians belonged the praise of original conception and execution. Whether it was owing to instinct or good fortune, they took the lead in every branch of mental cultivation; and even if, under the scourge of dire national calamities, they were in later times again and again outstripped in the race, still the germs of their creative powers lay latent among them, giving hope that some day, under more auspicious circumstances, the country to which strangers so readily allowed the vaunt of beauty, might reassert her titles to the distinction of "the Land of Genius."

Have these sanguine anticipations been realized? Has Italian genius during this first quarter of a century of national existence shown symptoms of its reviving powers? Is free Italy as great in art, literature, and science even as she was before Providence

struck the hour of her deliverance? Or is it true,
on the contrary, that to her first fit of political
exaltation a long spell of mental weariness and
languor, of what they call *marasma*, succeeded?

Alas! what avails even genius without the sense
which alone can direct its energies to a purpose,
and the strength of will that must bear it up
in the struggle through which the purpose may be
attained?

An Italian of the good old times struck out for
himself a new path in that realm of epic poetry over
which Homer had so long been sole sovereign. Where
the Latin had only attempted imitation, the Latin's
son rose to emulation, and reared a Gothic edifice in
every respect as wonderful as the primitive classical
structure. But the Divine Poem was not achieved
before many a year of unwearied labour had "worn
the poet to a thread." [1]

Again: another mediæval Italian steered his bark
across an unknown ocean, in quest of hidden con-
tinents; but he had first to overcome that human
stolidity with which "the gods themselves wrestled
in vain;" and in that struggle he had to waste the

---

[1] "E che m' ha fatto per più anni macro."
Dante, 'Paradiso,' xxv. 3.

best years of his life; and when he set out at last, it was with the determination to "find new worlds or be drowned."

As in Dante, as in Columbus, so in most other old Italians who achieved greatness, it will be found that loftiness of mind was associated with strength of backbone. Raphael for his short space of only thirty-seven years; Titian during his long spell of ninety-nine; Galileo with his "*Eppur si muove!*" Palestrina, the composer of music; Stradivarius, the maker of musical instruments, were all hard-working men; men of earnest purpose, wedded to their task, self-denying, long-enduring, convinced that "*Patiens dominabitur astris.*"

Is the race of such men extinct? Will the race revive? That the national character should have suffered from so long a period of enslavement and degradation as poor Italy had to go through is no more than could be expected. What is surprising is the apparent unconsciousness of this fact on the part of the people themselves; their inability or unwilling-ness to perceive and acknowledge that which is so obvious to their neighbours—that they have been for centuries, and even till yesterday, a fallen race; that they have, age after age, been distanced by rival

nations; and that to make up for lost time, to fit
themselves for their new destinies, and win back their
former place, it behoves them to be up and doing, to
be unremitting in their exertions, to work double
tides.

To impress the Italians with this necessity is no
easy task.   Unquestionably, as I had occasion to say
before, there is a considerable amount of work done
in Italy; and undoubtedly, also, that amount has
increased in this last score of years, even beyond the
rate of any augment of population.   The peasant in
the field, the artisan in the workshop, are as assiduous
in their employment as their too many Church and
State holidays will allow them to be.   The toil, as a
rule, is only too sadly out of proportion with the
bread it wins.   There are, besides, in every Italian
town, clusters of harmless but aimless *amateurs*, men
who dabble in literature or discourse on art, just as
young Dauphins took to locksmith's, or lovely Arch-
duchesses to dairy-maid's work—as an innocent way
to kill time.   But the work Italy is in need of is
something besides that of the mere drudge or of the
listless *dilettante*.   The Italians must be made to
love work for its own sake; for the energies, both
physical and moral, that it calls forth; for the

consciousness of power which it inspires ; for the lift it gives to the whole tone and temper of a man's character.

There is a wide-spread conviction among the present generation of Italians, that all of them have more or less borne a hand in "making" their country. It would be well if all of them would join in the effort by which the nation is to be "made." Surely this ought to be the first lesson of patriotism. But with the immense majority of the Italian people, it may be asserted that what is done is only half-hearted work. The old type of the Lazzarone earning his fifty centimes (5*d.*) by carrying a traveller's bag from the landing-place to the inn, and on the strength of those five pence managing to bask and sleep in the sun the livelong day, is becoming a rare bird in Naples itself. But it is by no means uncommon to meet a journalist who, on being told how fortunes are made in England by the Press, will ask how much a writer in a London paper may earn by a leading article ; and hearing that the remuneration is not unfrequently five guineas, he translates the sterling sum into something more than one hundred and thirty of his own lire, and exclaims, " *Per Bacco!* were I to come into possession of so much money

at one stroke, how long would it be ere the editor
would see my face again?"

Much of the sluggishness and indolence of this
fiacca or *fiaccona*, as they say in Italy, has been, as
we all know, laid to the charge of the enervating
climate. Life, it is argued, has unspeakable charm
in those sunny latitudes, and labour interferes with
its enjoyment. A Southerner loves idleness as he
loves life; and how abjectly he shrinks from death
may be inferred from the panic which the bare
mention of the cholera spread among those excitable
Latin multitudes, till the example of their noble King
showed them how strong a sense of duty will make a
man in a hospital ward as well as on a battle-field.
A nation which aspires to be great cannot afford to
shirk work, any more than it can allow itself to fear
death. A Southern people needs hardening; it
needs training like a war-horse, than which no
creature is by nature more nervous, yet none, when
more thoroughly broken, is more impetuously valiant.
It was proper education, it was discipline, that made
men as they were in Italy, and it is nothing else that
can again make them what they ought now to be.

It is a common saying that "an Italian will work
like any other man, if you will only make it worth

his while." And there is little doubt that an Italian labourer on a Swiss or Austrian railway will put up with heavier work and lighter wages than would satisfy an English navvy. But it is not merely to relieve present want, not merely for bread, that Italy should exert herself. Nor should her work be limited to the needy classes for whom the alternative lies between that and starvation. In Italy the worker should look to his country's honour for his reward. His stimulus should be the rehabilitation of her character, the revindication of her former supremacy. Her great men of olden times had indeed in many instances to work for daily bread. But the wages which they then earned, after ages have been paying ever since. Dante was not, while he wrote, much actuated by the thought of his copy-right; yet his book has made the fortune, we know not of how many publishers, commentators, and translators in all languages. Stradivarius sold his violins, most likely, at eight or ten ducats apiece; yet one of those marvellous fiddles will now fetch five hundred or a thousand guineas any day at a London auction. For the work of man's brain, like the juice of the grape, ripens and mellows by keeping. There are latent powers in it which, properly worked, may raise our achievements in after time far above any price that our grudging contemporaries may set upon them.

The workers who are at fault in Italy at the present day are those of the upper and middle classes. What stands in the way of intellectual development is over-education. The evil lies in those " High schools for the Million," of which we have given the enumeration in the foregoing chapter, the tendency of which is to bring forth a wretched mediocrity, through the throng of which no way is left for true eminence. The result, if no worse, is to break many a square peg in vain attempts to thrust them into as many round holes. For it takes a very clever master to guess which of the tools he is preparing for the world's work will turn out at all available, and a still cleverer to decide for what kind of work each tool may best be made available. A master, if himself a genius, may chance to detect genius in a Dante or a Stradivarius ; but in twenty cases to one he is likely to set a Stradivarius to string verses, and send a Dante to make violins ; the result a failure in each case.

There is hardly a youth in Italy who has not in his own town, near home, a gymnasium, lyceum, high school, academy, or conservatory, in which he may be made a doctor, an advocate, an engineer, or architect, an opera-singer or ballet-dancer, almost entirely free of expense. The matriculation and other fees, especially at the minor universities, are exceedingly low, and very usually remitted in the case of poor youths exhibiting more than ordinary talents, or distinguished by exemplary conduct. The examinations are conducted with more than paternal leniency, and new trials are allowed year after year, leaving the door open even for the most irreclaimable dunce. That same false humanity which makes an Italian jury shrink from the responsibility of condemning the most abandoned criminal to the gallows, makes an examining faculty loath to "*send down*" the most hopeless candidate. The sympathies of tender-hearted professors for the candidate, or the private solicitations of friends and relatives interested in his success, prevail over all considerations of the dignity of science and of the welfare of society; it makes the examiners utterly reckless of the dangers that life or property may run in the hands of M.D.s or LL.D.s who go through the course without the salutary dread of being "*plucked.*" The consequence is a general complaint in the country that the training of young men's minds in the High Schools is waning,

"Small by degrees and beautifully less;"

that graduates come up day by day who have never studied, and, what is worse, never acquired studious habits. The most indispensable thing for the development of the human understanding, and for the formation of a man's character, is that he should be suffered to find out his own way, and this cannot be practicable in a country where collegiate institutions, properly so called, and different from mere conventual establishments, can hardly be said to exist. A college in Italy is not, as it is in England, a little world apart, a small isolated community, a temporary home of its own, with its gates shut against all worldly distraction, against all social or domestic influence. The Italian student has his university almost in his own street, next door to his father's house. He studies in his class, but lives with his family. For a few hours of the morning or afternoon he may have college duties, but the remainder of the day is at his own disposal, and nothing interferes with his domestic habits or social engagements. He can freely frequent his *café*, his theatre, dividing his time between duty and pleasure like any other grown-up idle individual.

A distinction used to be drawn in former times at the Italian universities, between a mere auditor and a matriculated student, the latter being bound to report himself day by day to his professors, and expecting to be called to account for his proficiency. But with the ideas of "liberty, equality, and fraternity" there came up a prodigious relaxation of rule and discipline. The student, it was argued, is a rational, responsible being. He must clearly understand that it is for his own good to exert himself in those branches of learning which are to fit him for the career of his choice. It is best for him to learn what life is, at the same time that he fits himself for his profession.

A collegiate *esprit de corps* cannot spring up under such circumstances in an Italian student. He grows up all by himself, uninfluenced by constant contact with a good tutor, or by quickening intimacy with clever fellow-students, unstirred by that emulation which should have roused his energies, sobered his conceits, and made him know his place. The whole class he belongs to is a loose mob, frittering away their best years, reading bad novels, writing for worse newspapers, dabbling in politics, attending public meetings, holding meetings of their own, passing resolutions, getting up petitions and deputations; the university thus standing up as the head of a community of which it ought to be the hope; each

beardless undergraduate taking the lead in public
affairs; and that, strangely enough, in a country
where, by the letter of Charles Albert's written and
printed constitution, the very ablest statesman, a
Pitt himself, would not be admissible to the Lower
House, as deputy, before the age of thirty, nor to
the Upper House, as senator, before forty.

These organic vices in the system of university
education in Italy are sufficiently evident to all men
of sense. Father Curci, for one (a man early in life
a light among the Jesuits; more lately at open war
with the Papacy, and now, it seems, reconciled to it),
having made himself acquainted with the organization of the Oxford Colleges, had undertaken the
foundation of something of the same kind in his
own country; and with that view he had interested
the "Company," or Order of Jesus, to establish in
Pisa a college for young men of good family, who
should regularly join the university classes as
students, at lecture hours, having all the time a
home in their own college, subject to its rule and
discipline, under a rector, tutors, and proctors;
helped by them in their studies, and prepared for
the examinations; but above all things, guarded
against any dangerous doctrines emanating from

the professor's chair. In one word, the college was meant to supply the antidote to the university poison.

But all this could not be. The antagonism between Church and State forbade even the experiment. As a Jesuitical scheme, it was feared, perhaps with good reason, that the institution might prove a hot-bed of reactionary conspiracy, and the Government had from considerations of public security to put its veto upon the opening of the college, for which everything had been prepared, as Father Curci had already bought a large building, formerly a grand hotel, and made sure of the support and custom of conspicuous families.

Another man, Emilio Broglio (the very reverse of a Jesuit, one of the Moderate party, but with strong Conservative instincts), on being appointed Minister of Public Instruction in 1867, came into office with a firm determination to strike at the root of all scholastic abuses by introducing a sufficient degree of severity in the examinations, both at the earlier and later stages of the student's course, so as to send away at the end of it and for ever all the youths who gave no evidence of natural abilities, or of an earnest disposition to make the most of them. But either the Minister attempted too much at once, or the *fortiter in re* too absolutely prevailed in him over the *suaviter in modo,* or the evil had roots in the nation's disposition which no Ministerial good-will and firmness could reach—the upshot at all events was such an outcry against his *Draconian* measures on the part of the whole *scolaresca,* echoed by the alarmed parents and all other tender-hearted but feeble-minded persons, that the Minister, one of the most deserving Italian patriots and scholars, was denounced as a *Codino,* or re-actionist; that he was feebly supported and almost openly disavowed by his colleagues in the Chamber and Cabinet and threw up his portfolio, beaten but unconvinced, betaking himself to a literary work on Frederick II., King of Prussia; in his disappointment envying perhaps that absolute power which enabled a self-willed monarch to make men of his subjects in very spite of themselves.

That in spite of all these shortcomings in their educational methods, the Italian High Schools send forth men of talent in every branch of science, in letters and arts, it would be absurd to deny. For in Italy, as in other countries, there are those who understand that the student's real education begins on the day in which he leaves college. There are those who know that they must strive to make up at home for the time they have lost in class. But even many of these

are apt to limit their exertions to the bare exigencies
of their chosen profession. They think little of the
advantage of bringing a vast mass of accessory information to bear upon their knowledge of their special or
principal subject. They bring into their private study
that slackness and shallowness to which they were
long accustomed in their school-house. Their object
is merely to get on, through thick and thin, trusting
that where their acquaintance with theory is at fault,
practice may always be their safe guidance. In other
words, that if their work at the Medical School did
little towards making them doctors, walking the
hospitals may enable them to set up as general prac-
titioners; that a little pettifogging assurance may
avail them instead of that sound knowledge which
they failed to pick up at the Law Schools.

All we have said hitherto amounts merely to this,
that the Italian universities turn out a sufficient
number of physicians and surgeons, of attorneys and
barristers, some of them men of distinction, most of
them fit to carry on the business of curing or killing
their patients, of winning or losing their client's
law-suits.

This could not be otherwise. Italy must have her
own doctors and lawyers, just as she has her own

tailors and shoemakers. The only question is, whether Italy or any country is bound to bear the costs of the education of professional gentlemen; whether the State has a right to impose taxes on the whole people to bring up doctors and lawyers, while it leaves tailors or shoemakers to learn their trade at their parents' costs. And even much less reasonable it seems, that a tailor or shoemaker, who may be burdened with many sons, while he has to take upon himself all the trouble and expense about those whom he trains up in his own shop, or apprentices to a neighbour's trade, he should rid himself of the others by sending them to a State-supported university, and thus fitting them at the public charge for one of the so-called " liberal " professions.

High schools and academies, as well as technical, agricultural, and the like of these, are indeed highly desirable, or rather necessary institutions. But they should be self-supporting; indeed they can hardly be efficient on any other terms. And it is even questionable whether they have a right to exist on their own endowments, when either from insufficient means, or from the altered circumstances of their locality, they cease to answer the purposes which called them into being. Why Ferrara should have eighteen masters for only twenty-nine pupils, while the youths of that town and province may have all the advantages that Bologna and Padua offer them, either of them at little more than a score of kilometres distance by rail, is one of those things that cannot be easily understood, especially if we consider that even by clubbing together all the means of Ferrara, Padua, and Bologna, one could hardly collect such a staff of teachers, such a supply of libraries, museums, laboratories, etc., as in other countries are deemed indispensable to a first-rate university of the present day.

No doubt the idea of the extinction of these institutions, the foundation of some of which dates from the palmy days of the Este, of the Carrara, and other princely dynasties, must be repugnant to the local patriotism of those Italian cities; but it is the destiny of Italy that her present should rise from the *embarras des richesses* of her past. The cities themselves where those ancient schools had their rise are in many instances the mere skeletons of what they were. A slow but incessant decay brings many of the former glories of Italy to their inevitable end. The country must learn to bury its own dead. A nation cannot live on history alone.

The effect, besides, of a " cheap and nasty " instruction, held out to all classes of pupils by so many
High Schools and " Upper High Schools," is to choke
up every path to the " gentlemanly " professions with
a crowd of needy candidates, for whom, however deserving, it is not always possible to find profitable
employment. The community, even in Italy, cannot
consist only of doctors and lawyers, of painters and
sculptors, of opera-singers and ballet-dancers. There
is a great deal of work, of hard work, and even of
more or less dirty work, to be done in the world ;
work which no one would take up from choice,
were it not providentially ordained that it should fall
upon some one from necessity, and be suited to that
one's inclinations and abilities as well as to his inexorable circumstances. There will always be men
in the world born or made to be doctors, and men
doomed and only fit to be scavengers.

" *La carrière ouverte aux talents.*" To be sure. But
real genius will always know how to cut out a path
for itself, and of mere average talent every country
will always have considerably more than it needs.
The difficulty lies in finding the place a man may
most advantageously fill, to teach him to help himself
into it, and to sit contentedly in it. But the creation

of too many High Schools is apt to lead to very different, indeed to perfectly opposite results. It opens the careers to mediocrity; it awakens vague ambitions and encourages idle vanities; it fosters hopes the disappointment of which is sure to develop the seeds of all social disorders. It is quite possible to popularize, to *democratize* public instruction, till the university which was intended to be the training-ground of well-bred, polished gentlemen, is turned into a nursery of needy place-hunters, a mere *phalanstère* of beggars in broad-cloth and kid-gloves, and, what is worse, a hot-bed of insane and frothy, if not mischievous and riotous, political agitators.

The aim of Italian High Schools should be to rear not many, but able and reputable professional men. There are no doubt many such. There are, for instance, clever doctors in Italy; yet it is not often that the faith of foreign visitors, especially in the southern cities, is sufficiently strong to induce them to call in a native practitioner, even in the worst extremities. And, on the other hand, the Italians themselves will travel abroad any distance in cases where there is a possibility, as well as a necessity, of consulting a specialist, as if not trusting their own. This might be matter of mere prejudice, of *vogue* and fashion, but once the run was all the other way. The Italians, doctors or quacks, were the rage. And does not this in itself make it advisable to try to raise the credit of the Italian High Schools by diminishing their number, so as to concentrate and increase their efficiency? There is as much good talent as there is strong wine in Italy. To raise the reputation of either commodity, all that is needed is better care in the making and in fitting the produce for the market.

Nor should the object of Italian universities be wholly or exclusively utilitarian. Mere professionals whose proficiency in their particular branch of business is only carried on to the extent of insuring them a return in daily bread or a carriage and pair, cannot be looked upon as belonging to the category of intellectual men, or cultivators of science. The *raison d'être* of a real High School of the first rank, lies in its capacity to supply men whose main stimulus to exertion should be thirst for knowledge, delight in intense occupation, love of their fellow-beings, strong interest in the advancement of science, and in the indefinite improvement of their own mental faculties and acquirements.

In other words, the main purpose of a learner at a

High School should be work for its own sake. And with that view it would be well for Italy to have, not many such institutions, but only a few, or indeed even only one, but that one furnishing all the desirable means to the end.

CHAPTER III.

POETRY AND THE DRAMA.

Claims of the Italians to Intellectual Supremacy—Italian Literature —In the Opinion of Rival Nations—Judged by the Italians themselves—Poets—Dramatists—Tragic and Comic Writers— The Italian Language and its Dialects on the Stage—Popular Theatres—Italian Actors—Italian Mimicry—Decline of the Italian Opera.

IT would be too early to inquire what influence may as yet have been exercised on the condition of Italian literature by the scholastic or academical institutions referred to in the foregoing chapter. By far the greatest number of writers known to fame at home or abroad were born and grew up under the old dispensation. We must wait for the achievements of the generation rising under the new order of things, to be enabled to decide whether the great change which has given the Italians a country will open fresh fields for the enterprise of their national genius, and whether intellectual progress will keep pace with political advancement.

Up to the very close of the Napoleonic era, in 1815, Italy had still in Milan, Monti, Pindemonte and Foscolo, an acknowledged triumvirate of poets; she had an historian, Botta; a sculptor, Canova; a painter, Camuccini; a surgeon, Scarpa, and other men eminent in almost every branch of science. Nor had the lights gone out, nor were there any symptoms of perceptible decline in the early and less severe period of the Austrian domination. The Romantic school of Manzoni, Grossi, Berchet, etc. in Lombardy, and their Classic rivals, Niccolini in Tuscany, Leopardi in the southern provinces, upheld the standard of poetical composition in Italy almost to the level it reached in the lands of Schiller and Goethe, of Scott and Byron, of Victor Hugo and Lamartine. The Italians of this epoch, it is true, were not men of such transcendent powers as some of their Transalpine contemporaries; but they formed, as it were, an international guild and brotherhood with them. It must be borne in mind that the Peace of 1815 had given rise to an unprecedented liveliness of intercourse, and to a feeling of cordiality between the long estranged members of the European family. From England, from Germany, from Russia, notabilities of every description flocked to Italy, while

batches of political fugitives from that misgoverned
country were year by year driven to foreign shores
where a safe asylum and generous hospitality were extended to them. Those were the days when travellers
visited Italy attracted as much by sympathy with the
people as by admiration for the country. Intimacy
with distinguished Italians was sought by all men
with any pretension to learning, taste, and culture ;
Italian was studied as the fashionable language ;
Italian history supplied the themes for the poet, the
artist, the thinker of other lands ; and with the knowledge of the achievements of the Italians of former
ages grew the interest which won the noblest hearts
in behalf of the sufferings of the living generation.

There are many reasons why that lively interest
should now have considerably abated, and why the
Italians of the present day should be dealt by with
a sense of justice leaving but little room for tender
partiality and indulgence. Italy is now a free and
united country, a country with almost every element
of happiness, and with unmistakable yearnings after
greatness. From an object of compassion she has
all at once been raised to be an object of envy. Of
a nation to which so much has been given, it is but
natural that much should be expected. Gauged by

the measure of strict impartiality, it would be impossible to assert that intellectual progress has gone hand-in-hand in Italy with material development, and one of the many reasons may well be that the energies of the nation have been so thoroughly absorbed by the furtherance of the latter object, as to leave little leisure or inclination for the advancement of the former. "Politics," it has been asserted, "have killed literature."

The Italians, however, harbour far different views on the subject. They cannot be easily brought to admit the supposition of any considerable decline of mental activity in their naturally high-gifted race. Italy, in their conceit, is now as much the "land of genius" as she ever was; men of high distinction in every branch of literature and art are daily rising, and if their fame do not spread beyond the Alps, may it not (the Italians fancy) be owing to the envy and malice by which all neighbouring nations conspire to rob them of their due?

There is some strange misconception about this matter; other nations are perfectly willing to let the Italians be judged by some of themselves. The first January number of the London 'Athenæum' of each year publishes a statement of the conditions of

letters and arts in all civilized countries, and the
drawing up of those summaries is intrusted to such
of the able men in each of them as may be deemed
fittest to sit in judgment.   The task of supplying
that journal with a yearly account of the literary,
artistic, and scientific progress in Italy was for many
years assigned to Angelo de Gubernatis, and more
lately to Ruggero Bonghi, both of them diligent
scholars, and the latter conspicuous for uncommon
talent and information, for sound and calm judgment,
and for warm, honest patriotism—the leading man in
the literature of the day.

Well, the reports published year by year by these
gentlemen of such works as appear in print in various
parts of their country, are not calculated to give
foreigners a very exalted idea of the present energy
of the Italian intellect; nor are the essays on the
conditions of contemporary literature published by
Amedée Roux or Luigi Capuana very likely to raise
the common run of Italian living authors to a much
higher rank in the world's estimation.

The poets enjoying the greatest popularity in Italy
after the death of Giusti, Prati, Aleardi, and other
actors or spectators of the great national struggle, are
Giosuè Carducci (Enotrio Romano), born near Pietra-

santa in Tuscany, now professor at Bologna; Mario
Rapisardi, a native of Catania; and Olindo Guerrini
(Lorenzo Stecchetti), of Ravenna.

The first of the three, Carducci, is unquestionably the
poet of the age. He has a manly and vigorous, grand
and trenchant, though unequal and laboured manner
of his own, and not unfrequently rises to the highest
flights of lyrical inspiration. His earliest verses were
prompted by generous patriotic instincts; but he
took an ultra-Mazzinian view of his country's politics,
and inveighed in a savage style against the *baseness*
of the practical men who were fortunate enough to
accomplish Mazzini's object by other means than
those Mazzini's school approved of, and the charge
of *cowardice* which, in his opinion, the Moderates
(Opportunists, Possibilists, and other adversaries of the
Irredentists) deserved, was by him extended to the
whole of his countrymen, with an extremely narrow
exception of the Mazzinian and Garibaldian heroes.[1]
He seemed to cool down a little in his political

[1] "Accoglietemi, udite, o degli eroi
   Esercito gentile :
   Triste novella io recherò tra voi :
   La nostra patria è vile."

'In Morte di Giovanni Cairoli,' 'Giambi ed Epodi,' di Giosuè
Carducci, Bologna, 1882. New Edition, p. 79.

enthusiasm, but he was unshaken in his hostility to
all religion, both revealed and natural, and he com-
pressed all his atheism into a little poem of fifty little
stanzas (two hundred lines of five syllables each),
which is held in honour in Italy as the most success-
ful of his metrical effusions.   This is the famous
'Hymn to Satan,' in the hero of which the poet
recognizes the incarnation of that modern science
which, in his expectation, is destined to demolish
the whole edifice of human belief, doing away with
the idea of a personal Deity itself.

Carducci apostrophizes Satan [1] as "the boundless
principle of existence"; he calls him "Matter and
Spirit, Sensation and Reason," a Power engaged in
a life-and-death antagonism with God, whom the
poet scouts as the mere vague creation of man's
helpless ignorance and abject cowardice.   In this
strife Satan (whose name is used as synonymous with
Science, with Rebellion, and the Avenging Power of
Reason) enlists on his side the whole legion of Christian

---

[1] " A te, dell' Essere
   Principio immenso,
   Materia e Spirito
   Ragione e Senso."

 'Inno a Satana,' Carducci, ' Levia Gravia.' Bologna, 1881. New
Edition, p. 127.

reformers, Abailard, Arnold of Brescia, Savonarola, and Martin Luther, and at their head succeeds in establishing that "free thought" which is eventually to overcome the Jehovah of the priests.[1]

Enlarging, if not improving on this idea of the perpetual warfare between Reason and Authority, this idea of a struggle between Matter and Spirit (whether one and the same substance, or two substances blended together and co-existing throughout the whole period of time and the whole mass of the universe), Carducci's contemporary, Mario Rapisardi, in an allegorical poem of fifteen cantos, in blank verse (a

[1]   " Gittò la tonaca
        Martin Lutero :
        Gitta i tuoi vincoli
        Uman pensiero.
            E splendi e folgora
        Di fiamme cinto ;
        Materia, inalzati ;
        Satana ha vinto.
            .   .   .   .
            Salute, o Satana,
        O Ribellione,
        O forza vindice
        Della Ragione !
            Sacri a te salgano
        Gl' incensi e i voti !
        Hai vinto il Géova
        De i Sacerdoti."
            ' Inno a Satana,' pp. 135, 137.

volume of four hundred pages), describes the same conflict, at the end of which the hero, not Satan, but Lucifer, the "Bearer of Light," accomplishes the conquest and the annihilation of the Deity.

Mixing up the old myth of Prometheus, and the vital spark smuggled from heaven, with the Temptation Scene in the third chapter of the Book of Genesis, Rapisardi makes his hero start from the Caucasus (leaving the son of Japetus chained to the rock, with the vulture gnawing at his liver), and bound on a long campaign against that Divine phantom which, owing to man's disregard of his own reason, had for ages enthralled the deluded minds of Adam's descendants in degrading superstitions. As the friend of man from the beginning, this Light-bearing hero becomes the constant attendant of the various tribes of the human family, throughout all the historical phases by which their intellectual emancipation is ultimately accomplished. He is present at the English, the American, and the French Revolutions; hovers about the battle-fields of Solferino, Sadowa, and Sédan, as well as at the battering and breaching of the Roman wall at Porta Pia; and, at the end of this marvellous hash of grand human episodes, he places himself at the

head of the great thinkers of the Rousseau and
Voltaire school, and makes ready for the final con-
test. He drives before him the champions of the
Church, Torquemada, Dominic Guzman, Ignatius
Loyola, Pius V., Sixtus V., and the whole host of
the saints and angels of darkness, and at last storms
in his last ditch, in the deepest hole of the earth,
that nondescript, invisible, intangible, fabulous Being,
which, under a variety of denominations, of Jehovah,
Jove, Allah, Bramah, etc., has been for so many
centuries the bugbear of mankind.

Lucifer's weapon throughout the conflict has been
only a ray of light. This blissful beam he now turns
upon the shapeless and unsubstantial, yet Proteiform
Being which cowers before it, which goes out smoking,
fizzing, and hissing like red-hot iron in cold water,
or lime slaked in water or vinegar. And " this was
the end of the Eternal ! "

The war at an end, the exulting conqueror makes
his way back to the snowy Caucasus, and stands
before Prometheus, bidding him "rise and rejoice,
for the great tyrant is slain ! " [1]

[1]   " Toccollo
De l'acuto suo raggio, e a parte a parte
Lo trapassò. Stridea, come rovente
Ferro immerso ne l'onda, il simulacro

It is difficult to imagine the purpose these young poets, whom the Italian Government trusts with the task of the development of youthful minds from their professors' chairs, hope to fulfil by dwelling on this glorious victory of Reason and Science over Religion. It is on their part a vain wish, a delusion. For they ought to see that their success is as yet not complete nor insured, that all monks are not unfrocked because Luther was, nor have the priests of St. Januarius been yet starved out from want of votaries at their miraculous shrine. Satan is not yet king, though the Pope is dethroned; and the number of "fools" that really say in their hearts "there is no God,"

Fuggitivo del Nume; e a quella forma
Che crepitando si scompone e scioglie
Fumigante la calce a l'improvviso
Tasto de l'acqua o del mordente aceto,
Tale al raggio del Ver struggeasi il vano
Fantasma; e in vapore indi converso,
Tremolando si sciolse,. e all' aria sparve.
　　Così moría l'Eterno: Ai consüeti
Balli movean gli antichi astri; dal cielo
Luminoso partian come in trionfo
Le magne ombre de i sofi, e a tutti innanzi
Lucifero: Arrivò col sol novello
Su 'l Caucaso nevato, ove al soffrente
D'adamantino cor figlio di Temi,
—Levati, disse, il gran Tiranno è spento."

　　Rapisardi, 'Lucifero,' *Poema*, Milan, 1877, p. 395.

is not large, though only too many live as if such were their conviction. Do these poets, who in their championship of blank unbelief trust to the charm of rhyme rather than to the strength of reason, fancy that the Italians, or any other people, would be much wiser or better even if it could be mathematically demonstrated that " God is a phantom " ? Did even Carlyle irrevocably establish the fact that the Pope is an " Old Chimera " ? Faith is not so easily demolished, nor can any edifice be built on the mere quicksands of doubt. Do away with Jehovah and Satan, and men will still ask, " What remains ? "

The answer of the Satanic school may be : " Pleasure, happiness, the delight of eating, drinking, and being merry, for to-morrow we die." But is man vile enough to adopt a mere gospel of self-indulgence ? Has all this preaching of the emancipation of reason no better aim than the gratification of brutal passion ? There are episodes in Rapisardi's ' Lucifero ' which, to say nothing of the irreverence of things held sacred by the multitude, must strike even the most sceptic readers or most lenient critics as not only too gross and grotesque, but too wantonly obscene, too gratuitously offensive to every shadow of bare decency and good taste.

A tendency to shock common decency by the exhibition of sensualism in poetry, as by an excessive display of the *nudo* in painting, is rapidly gaining ground in Italy, nor is it, to say the truth, merely and wholly an importation of the literary and artistic manner now prevalent in the so-called Realistic French school. It is, unfortunately, an old school in Italy, for it has flourished from Boccaccio down to Casti, Pananti, and worse. But no one, perhaps, more recklessly sinned in that respect than the third in that triumvirate of Italian poets I have named, Guerrini, in whose verses there undeniably is much of the Anacreontic grace and elegance of language, but who has gone perhaps farther in his cynicism than he feared might suit the taste of Italian readers ; those readers whom, probably for that reason, he mystified with the assumption of a feigned name, giving out his book as the posthumous collection of the poems of an imaginary cousin, Lorenzo Stecchetti.[1]

I am not here assuming the authority of a critic or a moralist ; I only try to account for the fact that the Italian poetry has hitherto made but little headway into foreign countries, and least of all into

[1] 'Postuma, Canzoniere, e Nuova Polemica, versi di Lorenzo Stecchetti,' Bologna, 1882.

England; for it does not seem fit for translation, and it is not, fortunately, very intelligible to English readers in the original.

Nothing, meanwhile, is more striking than the godlessness and licentiousness of these rhyme-smiths of emancipated Italy, especially if we reflect that they are the sons and grandsons of that Romantic school of Manzoni, and of those fellow-sufferers of Pellico, Confalonieri, and other martyrs of Spielberg, whose meek piety and resignation, and faith without hope, were so much stronger than the bayonets and dungeons of their oppressors; and whose religion was merely a natural revulsion of feeling against the arrogant philosophy that the French Jacobinism of a former period had forced upon Italy at the sword's point. Thus blindly and fitfully do the vagaries of the human mind proceed through successive and alternate fits and starts of action and reaction; and so true it is that nations are as sure to be reminded of God in their affliction, as they are apt to forget Him in their exultation of success.

It would be needless in a work of this nature to give even the names of the score or two of minor poets now living, or recently dead, whose reputation has yet hardly gone beyond the limits of the town or

province where themselves or their verses first saw
the light. In Italy, as elsewhere, few are the students
who do not in their green years try their hands at
that kind of work. But the sober-minded among
them soon learn that mediocrity in song is an abomin-
ation in the eyes of God and man. Some of them
betake themselves to other branches of literature.
Others devote themselves to law or physics, politics
or the press, to more useful or reputable, but, at all
events, less famishing pursuits.

More regard should be shown to Italian lady poets,
some of whom rose to distinction as valiant defenders
of those bulwarks of morality, the foundations of
which are being rashly sapped by their male contemporaries, and who stand up for those domestic
virtues which ought to be the certain evidence of
patriotic worth.

First of these may be mentioned Erminia Fuá-
Fusinato, a Venetian, and a born Jewess, but won over
to the Christian faith by Ruth-like conjugal devotion
—a woman of Titianic beauty, not long ago cut off
by early death in Rome, where she had devoted herself to the cause of superior female education. With
true woman's instinct this lovely being endeavoured
to soothe the aggrieved manes of Giacomo Leopardi,

making up for the loveless life to which, in the shy consciousness of personal deformity, the unfortunate poet doomed himself, by her noble strains tendering all her warm and ardent sympathy to the great departed, at the same time that she upbraided him for the want of faith which blinded him to the readiness for self-sacrifice and genius-worship on which he should have reckoned in his intercourse with her sex. Equally genuine poetical assurances of posthumous love were addressed to the misanthropic bard by his townswoman, Alinda Brunamonte, perhaps the most *simpatica* of Italian poetesses now living.

With these should be named Rosina Muzio Salvo, Concettina Fileti, Mariannina Coffa-Caruso, Grazia Pierantoni-Mancini, and last, not least, the *improvvisatrice* Giannina Milli, all of them blameless wives and exemplary mothers, who remind us how general it was, in former ages in Italy, to find women whose gifts of genius were associated with loftiness of character and purity of life—women of the stamp of Vittoria Colonna, Veronica da Gambara, Gaspara Stampa, Olimpia Morata.

A style of poetry which has been lately cultivated in Italy with signal success is the Drama; very naturally, in a country where readers and purchasers of

books are not many, and the frequenters of the
theatres are legion, and where the play-wright in a
great measure depends on the play-actor for success,
and comes in for at least a small share of the profits ;
where, besides, the poet's fame follows the fortunes of
his actor's troupe all over the country, as they stroll
from town to town. The greatest dramatist of the
day, Pietro Cossa, a Roman, first became known for
his treatment of classical subjects, ' Nerone,' ' Messa-
lina,' 'Giuliano l'Apostata,' ' Sordello,' etc. ; but his
most loudly applauded, though hitherto unpublished,
performance after his ' Nerone ' was by some considered
'I Napoletani del 1799'—an exhibition of the grievous
scenes of that ruthless Bourbon reaction against French
Republicanism in which Nelson and Lady Hamilton
played so conspicuous a part.

A more ambitious dramatist, and known above
several others, is Felice Cavallotti, a man distinguished from early youth as an author in various
branches of Italian literature, and more lately as a
brilliant orator in the Chamber of Deputies, where
he stands up as an out-and-out champion of the
most advanced Radical ideas. To his early dramas,
' I Pezzenti' (the *Gueux*), 'Guido,' and 'Agnese,' he
has more lately added ' Alcibiade,' which still holds

his ground on the stage, but which loses much of
its prestige in a cold private perusal. Considerable
success has been achieved this year, 1886, by his
'Figlia di Jefte.' Even on the stage, however, it is
doubtful whether any of his pieces, or of those of any
other living dramatists, may hope to enjoy the public
favour which was so constantly and for so many years
bestowed on Pellico's 'Francesca da Rimini.'

Greater success have achieved in Italy the comic
poets, at the head of whom have been for some
time Paolo Ferrari and Gherardo del Testa, the
former a Modenese, the other a Tuscan. Ferrari
came out in 1852 and 1857 with his 'Goldoni e le
sue Sedici Commedie' and 'Parini e la Satira,' both
works of greater merit than any of his later comedies,
'Le due Dame,' 'Cause ed effetti,' 'Il Suicidio,' 'Il
Duello,' 'Il Ridicolo,' some of which foundered
wofully, even on the scenes of his own dear Milan,
the city where he resides, and where he is treated
with especial benevolence. The reputation of Gherardi
del Testa, recently deceased, seemed better grounded.
His latter pieces, 'La vita nuova,' 'Il vero Blasone,'
'Oro e orpello,' 'La Carità pelosa,' 'Le Coscienze
Elastiche,' etc., still go the round of the Italian stage ;
so do those of Giacometti, 'La Morte Civile,' 'Il

Poeta e la Ballerina,' etc.; those of Giacosa, 'La
Partita a Scacchi,' 'It Trionfo d'Amore,' 'Il fratello
d'armi,' etc.; those of Suner, 'I Legittimisti,' 'Ogni
lasciato è perso,' 'Chi ama teme,' etc.; those of
Torelli, whose 'Trionfo dei Mariti,' a great success,
was followed by more or less clamorous defeats.
More popular are the Proverbs, one or two act
pieces, of De Renzis and Ferdinando Martini: those
of this latter, 'L'Uomo propone e la Donna dispone,'
'Chi sa il giuoco non l'insegni,' etc. are the delight
of amateur performers throughout Italy. All these
and many more prolific authors evince great anxiety
to minister to the craving for novelty of the
fastidious and capricious Italian public, by trying
their hands at new subjects and in various styles of
composition; thus, like their brethren in Spain, in
England, in Germany, striving (not always successfully) to stand up for their original national theatre,
and to roll back the invading tide of good or bad
French pieces incessantly smuggled in by professional
bunglers (*guastamestieri*) in clumsy translations, imi-
tations, and adaptations.

The Italian writers for the stage, however, especially the comic writers, who choose their subjects
from· modern popular life, labour under this sad

disadvantage, that they use a literary language, such
as none of their *Dramatis Personæ*, high or low,
would speak in their familiar real-life intercourse.
It is this unfortunate circumstance which gives the
style of all Italian writers, both in prose and verse,
that somewhat stiff and stilted artificial manner
which is natural to all who attempt to express
themselves in a dead or an acquired tongue ; but the
awkwardness is especially felt in the dialogue, both
of serious and comic pieces, where what the actor
delivers in Italian is merely the translation of what
he thinks and would say in his own Piedmontese,
Milanese, or other unwritten and almost *unwritable*
patois. This unfortunate partiality of the Italians of
all classes for their uncouth, however lively, humourous, and expressive dialects, used even by persons of
the highest rank (the king and queen not excepted),
is not one of the least serious hindrances, not only
to the development of a plain and natural diction in
any style of composition, and of a heartfelt and forcible
utterance in forensic or parliamentary debates (whence
the dialects are banished), but also to the spread of
a practical medium for the instruction of the lower
classes, who to the end of their lives speak Italian
at the best as the half-educated Welsh speak English.

It is one of the evil customs of old Italy, which the school-master now abroad, and the inevitable exigencies of a united public free life, are gradually but by no means rapidly tending to reform, though it is rather to be wished than it can be hoped, that they will "reform it altogether." For what concerns the stage, the unfitness of the Italian, especially for the comic dialogue, was felt from the very rise of those ' Commedie dell' Arte,' where either the dialogue was not written but only sketched, as the Welsh speeches of Owen Glendower and Lady Mortimer in Shakespeare's ' First Part of Henry the Fourth ; ' or in which the masks, Pantaloon, Brighella, Harlequin, etc., all spoke in the low dialects prevalent in their respective provinces. The difficulty was equally experienced by Goldoni, whose most telling comedies of ' I Rusteghi,' ' Le Baruffe Chiozzotte,' etc. were all written in his own boneless yet racy Venetian ; and it is evident at the present time in the delight which not only Italians of all parts of the country, but even utter strangers from other lands, and totally unacquainted with either language or dialects, find in the performances of Gianduia in Turin, of Meneghino in Milan, and till lately of the San Carlino troupe in Naples, where hardly one word of pure Italian is uttered, except by some fantastic, affected personage, whose *Lingua Toscana in bocca Romana* is made fun of by the rest of the company as something ostentatious and outlandish. Not a few of these provincial theatres have ceased to exist; but some of the strolling companies, playing in the various dialects, still receive the applause of the most civilized Italian cities.

Among the plays in the vulgar vernacular that had the longest run on the stage are those of the Piedmontese Pietracqua, Garelli, Zoppis, and Toselli; the last-named also an unrivalled actor, lately deceased, for many years the soul of the D'Angennes Theatre in Turin. But none of their pieces ever achieved such wonderful success as those of Vittorio Bersezio, and especially his 'Monsu Travet,' a semi-tragic, wholly pathetic, humourous play (the character of the Protagonist acted by the above-named Toselli), describing the sorrows of a hard-working, much-bullied, ill-paid *impiegato*, or clerk in a Government office, one of the victims of that hag Bureaucracy, who, however maternally she may deal with the upper class of public functionaries, shows herself a most ruthless stepmother to the poor fags of the lower ranks of the service.

F 2

Bersezio, an accomplished writer, who has attained distinction in various branches of his craft, attempted a reproduction in Italian of his popular Piedmontese play. But the translation ('Le disgrazie del Signor Travetti') fell flat even in those theatres of Florence and Rome where the original patois, though little understood, had been most enthusiastically applauded—a very irrefragable evidence that for genuine pathos as well as for spontaneous humour, those provincial dialects, being the real mother-tongue, possess powers not easily transfused into the always too unfamiliar national language. For the same reason the 'Fuggitiva,' a metrical romance which Tommaso Grossi wrote both in Italian and in his own Milanese dialect, draws, in this latter form, scalding tears from eyes which all the elegance of the Italian version leaves dry.

To an Italian writer even of the greatest merit, his national language is but the gala coat that a good land labourer only wears on the Sunday or holiday. The tailor may fit him never so admirably, his own instinct and careful study may give his use of it both elegant ease and infinite grace, but the garment will never sit so comfortably on him as his own every-day working jacket.

For what concerns the stage, however, the thought suggests itself, that the success of all Italian dramatic works, not excepting these dialectical pieces, may in a great measure be due rather to the actors than to the authors of them. The fame of Italian stage-players flies now much further than that of Italian play-writers. One sees large Russian, English, and American audiences thrilled by the mere tone of voice, look, and gesture of Rossi, Salvini, Ristori, and others (all pupils of Gustavo Modena, as he was of his father, Giacomo), though by far the greatest number of those enraptured spectators, even *libretto* in hand, can but catch here and there a word or an idea of an action before them. The expression of countenance and the vehemence of passion of a Southern race enable an Italian to dispense with utterance on the stage as well as in real life. They *look* what they wish, but deem superfluous, to say. And there never was anything more marvellous than the effect of those " Dramas without words," called ' Pantomime,' or ' Balli Pantomimici,' such as ' La Vestale,' 'Gabriella di Vergy,' etc.—acting ballets which reached perfection on the vast stage of La Scala, in Milan, under the management of Viganò, and with such artists as Molinari, La Pallerini, and others to set them off.

Such dumb-show spectacles, aided by all the charms
of gorgeous scenery and costume and select music,
for more than one season gave reason to the opera to
tremble for its wonted command of the Italian stage.

All this, however, ballet, opera, and anything else
connected with the stage, of which the Italians once
claimed the monopoly, belongs to the past. Verdi
himself, now above seventy years old, though still
living, and preparing a new ' Othello ' for La Scala,
in Milan, has hardly ever been the composer he was
since Cavour had him returned as a Deputy to the
first Italian Chamber in Turin in 1860, when he
ceased to be a Maestro, though he never took to
politics. For many years he had been enjoying his
otium cum dignitate in the neighbourhood of his birth-
place near Busseto, in the province of Parma, only
coming out with reluctance in 1871, when he gave
the ' Aïda ' to the Egyptian stage.

As to the new composer, the Wagnerite, Arrigo
Boito, he, as well as the other Boito, Camillo, takes
place among the Italian writers of the day. But his
operas, of which he supplies the words as well as the
notes, do not seem to be such spontaneous productions, or at least are not so frequent as those by
which Bellini or Donizetti met year by year the

incessant demands of the *Impresarios* of a former epoch.

There is still an opera in Italy. The Milan, Naples, and other *conservatorios*, still turn out young composers, singers, and dancers by the score. But poor Italy is reduced to the condition of a half-bankrupt pastry-cook or confectioner, compelled to eat his own dainties, in the utter hopelessness that the old trade will ever bring paying customers to his shop.

It is not perhaps merely the caprice of fashion that has to such great extent and by so sudden and strange a reaction deprived the Italian melo-drama of the Paris, London, and St. Petersburg patronage. One would say that the creative genius of Rossini's countrymen has come to a sudden collapse; as if there were no longer a possibility of hitting upon melodies that are not mere reminiscences of those which are already the stock-in-trade of itinerant barrel-organ boys.

Possibly, also, the Italians are still smarting under the taunt too often thrown in their faces, that they were a nation of mimes and zanies, of fiddlers and daubers. Perhaps they are bent on proving that, if they can be no better than that, they had rather be *nothing*.

CHAPTER IV.

ROMANCE AND HISTORY.

Novels and Plays in Italy—Light and Serious Literature—Political Literature — The Italian Press — Pamphlets — Historical and Biographical Literature—Local and General History—National and Foreign History—Italian and Foreign Scholarship—Italian Reverence and Hospitality to Foreign Learned Men.

THERE are many reasons why the Italians should not hitherto have favoured Romance to the same extent as they encouraged the Drama. In the first place they are dwellers in cities. They are, as a rule, no great readers, and fiction will probably never be to them so dear a luxury as it is to the home-in-the-country-loving Northerners; for reading would never make up for that social intercourse which is the chief recommendation of an Italian theatre. The Italians are an eminently gregarious people, and a book, however amusing, is not one of the pleasures easily enjoyed in company. By sitting at a play, moreover, an Italian not only spares his bright eyes, but gives

them and his ears at the same time all the treat that
the accessories of the *mise en scène* add to the interest
of the piece before him. With respect to the "corrupting influence" of either style of literature (*n'en
deplaise* Jean-Jacques Rousseau), a novel can do as
much mischief as a play.

In the trade of novelists the Italians only came
forth as imitators. Foscolo and Manzoni, of course,
could have written 'Iacopo Ortis,' and 'I Promessi
Sposi,' even if 'Werther' and any of the 'Waverley
Novels' had never appeared. But the whole chorus
of Manzoni's contemporaries, Grossi, Cantù, Rovani,
Baozzni, Varese, D'Azeglio, Carcano, Rossini, Guerrazzi, etc., would perhaps never have seen the light
had not the Wizard of the North struck out for
himself a new path in the literature of fiction, in which
the dullest as well as the brightest intelligence found
it possible to go after—a very long way after him ;
for the hope of success in this hybrid style of composition rests on the delusive notion that fact may
supply the basis for an edifice of which the builder's
inventive powers will only have to plan the super-
structure, the labour being thus halved—a mistake
which Walter Scott himself found out too late, and
which ended by deterring his staunchest imitators

from their work. Among the disappointed ones
was probably Massimo d'Azeglio, the fragments of
whose unfinished narrative,. 'La Lega Lombarda,'
have lately been published merely out of reverence
for the memory of the patriot and statesman best
entitled among his countrymen to the appellation of
the *Chevalier sans Reproche.* With those eight chapters
on which the author's pen fell, probably owing to his
conviction that God's history is never more romantic
than when least tampered with by man's fiction, we
shall, let us hope, hear no further mention of Italian
historical novels.

But there is, on the other hand, no lack of Italian
novelists who look for subjects among the ordinary
incidents of actual life, and attempt pictures of characters, manners, and costumes of the living generation, especially among the middle and lower classes ;
and some of them seek or create their heroes among
the least known populations of the southern provinces
in the mountain and marshes, and along the shores,
of Naples, Sicily, or Sardinia.

The first specimen of a tale from every-day life,
'Angiola Maria,' by Giulio Carcano, came out as
early as 1839. But since that date both Carcano
himself, to his last day (his death was recorded very

lately), and a whole legion of others, many of them
still young rising authors, have devoted themselves
to the same kind of writing ; and with such success,
that in a recent review of some of their works it
has been frankly asserted, that " in the domains of
fiction, at least, the Italians can measure themselves
with their European contemporaries, and not be
found wanting." [1] Of many of these, however, barely
the names have ever been heard abroad, and of only
very few has the translation been attempted or found
practicable. And this for a variety of reasons, and
especially because in Italy itself neither a writer nor
a publisher would venture on the production of a
three-volume novel, for the purchasers of books in
that country are very few, and the circulating libraries,
on which an English novelist almost entirely reckons
for the sale of his works, are well-nigh unknown south
of the Alps, the only one on a large scale being that
of Viesseux in Florence—a foreign institution, and
mainly relying on English subscribers for existence.

Italian novelists in most cases limit themselves to
one volume *novelettes* and sketchy tales, contributed
as *feuilletons*, or appendices to the newspapers, in

[1] 'A Quartette of Italian Novelists,' Blackwood's Magazine,
January, 1885, page 72.

competition with indifferently translated foreign
works in the same style, of which at least ten French
appear for one taken from English, German, or other
originals.

Fiction in Italy has thus to contend with the same
difficulties as encompass the stage, especially the
comic stage. The most serious is the above-hinted
baneful influence of the overwhelming *farrago* of
French novels. With a view to counteract these
terrible evils, some of the best Italian writers, it
is true, have often looked for their models among
the productions of other nations; but they have had
to contend with unfamiliar languages, and such
differences of feelings, habits, and ideas as rendered
the translation or merely the understanding of the
original a very arduous task. One of the most
popular story-tellers of the present day, for instance,
is Salvatore Farina, a native of Sorso near Sassari
in Sardinia, and he goes by the name of the "Italian
Dickens"; but by the side of him must be placed
Giovanni Verga and Luigi Capuana (two of them), to
both of whom the unenviable appellation of "Italian
Zola" has been applied, while Matilde Serao, a
Neapolitan, has been hailed by a French critic as
"La petite George Sand." No very high claims to

originality these, if we remember that sixty years
ago the highest eulogy that was attributed to Sir
Walter Scott was to be addressed by the Italians as
"the Ariosto of the North." Verily the tables are
turned !

The consequence of this all-flooding tide of French
literature is, that in many a case of these Italian
pictures of pretended Italian manners the reader has
merely a jumble of bright rosy or deep black, but all
exaggerated hues—a strange exhibition of unblemished
democratic heroism by the side of unmitigated aristocratic blackguardism; both the virtues of the lower
and the villainy of the upper classes standing out
in impossible contrast—a picture of tints not natural,
of forms and features and characters not indigenous,
a mere French travesty of Italian life, in which one
sees the French *falsa riga* or ruling paper through
the thin tissue of every Italian page, the style
outlandish, the language shockingly bastardized.

In Italy, as elsewhere, the all-engrossing theme
of romance is Love ; but unfortunately in French as
well as in Frenchified Italian society (as novelists
describe it) all lawful love appears as a flat, flavour-
less dish, hardly as tempting in all its freshness and
purity, when served up with the bride-cake as dessert

at the close of the wedding-breakfast, as it is when
snatched as a forbidden dainty, with the evil bloom
of a stolen fruit upon it.   The very best of wives in
these novels, you would say, is to her lawful husband
only a woman ; the angel is his neighbour's wife.

It is for this reason, perhaps, that some of the best
Italian novelists take by preference their subjects
from those lower social orders where the Seventh
Commandment is less generally, less inevitably
broken ; where feelings are more genuine and earnest,
and the passions, though violent, less perverse and
at cross purposes ; where the love romance leads to
rather than starts from the marriage ceremony.
Some of Salvator Farina's masterpieces, for instance,
'Oro Nascosto,' 'Amore ha cent 'occhi,' etc., exhibit
strong but upright characters, from the primitive
population of his native island.   The best stories
appearing under the borrowed name of Marchesa
Colombi (a lady whose real name is Torelli-Viollier,
nata Torriani), 'In Risaia,' 'Il tramonto di un Ideale,'
etc., describe scenes from the fever-haunted rice-
grounds of the rich marshy flat where Lombardy
borders on Piedmont.   And Matilde Serao's 'Leg-
gende Napoletane' are written from her own experiences of the lower population of that noisiest and

most impulsive of Italy's cities. So likewise in Verga's 'Don Gesualdo,' 'I Malavoglia,' 'La Vita de' campi,' etc., the scene is laid among the fishermen of the Sicilian coast—a rugged, struggling, suffering, but by no means debased or uninteresting set of human beings.

The drawback is that these poor personages, taken from the humbler spheres of the people, have an utterance of their own, and that is seldom if ever introduced into a novel any more than on the stage. In Italy, as we have seen, Italian is nowhere the common people's language, not even in Florence, whose dialect, by far purer than any other, appears as it really is, only in some of the humourous writings of Yorick, the *nom de plume* under which Piero Ferrigni, a clever journalist, now and then chooses to appear in print. Were a novelist to make his popular heroes speak in their own vernacular idioms, his story would in many cases be barely understood at ten or twenty miles' distance from the spot where the scene lies. How could a Roman, for instance, any more than a Dutchman, ever guess that *El prestin di scansc*, in Milanese, means in Italian, "Il forno delle grucce"? How could a Florentine make out that *Ans' sem gnan vist* is Parmesan for "Non ci siamo nè anche veduti"?

or that in the jargon of Pavia (lately quoted by
'Fanfulla') *Coup' i gaï, e paccia i poï*, must be inter-
preted " Ammazza i galli e mangia i polli ? "

In a style of literature, in which, since Walter
Scott, the dialogue is the very soul of the action,
how can the illusion be kept up, if almost every
word spoken is as unnatural as was the sound con-
veyed through a *porte-voix* mask on the ancient
stage, to enable the performer's voice to reach the
most distant rows of a very large audience ?

On the stage, if we do not understand the actor's
speech, we may at least see his countenance, but in
a dumb book we can only make out what we read,
and the dialogue is not natural so long as it has
to go through a translation. We accept translation
as a matter of necessity, so long as the hero is an
ancient or an alien personage.   But with one of our
own people, with a Caleb Balderstone or an Andrew
Fairservice, with a Fagin or an Artful Dodger, any
other utterance than the Lowland Scotch of the former,
or the Attic Cockney of the latter, would sound so
unreal as to cause more than half the spirit of the
dialogue to fall flat.   It is not in the *Della Crusca*
language that a coal-heaver or a rail-splitter should
speak, and yet it is in that language that an Italian

novelist perforce makes all his personages, high or low, equally discourse. His dialogue is as much a translation as would be that of some of Scott's or Dickens's novels in the Italian garb in which Barbieri or Borsieri clothed them, and which the Italians can only relish on the principle that "half a loaf is better than no bread."

There is, nevertheless, in the farrago of novels and minor tales with which Italy is inundated, and for the mere names of whose authors room could hardly be afforded in these pages, very sufficient evidence of every variety of genuine talent. We will say nothing as to genius, for that is too rare a plant in all ages and countries, and it sprouts up, as the wind bloweth where it listeth; it grows up, alone or in clusters, as the stars shine in the firmament, amenable to no atmospheric influence, affected by no rain or drought, by no fitful change of the seasons.

Of the bright galaxy that gladdened the first half of the nineteenth century, light after light had gone out before the second birth of the Italian nation. But that was not the case in Italy alone. Like Manzoni and Foscolo, Byron and Scott, Goethe and Schiller left blanks not easily filled up. And of their few survivors, Victor Hugo, Carlyle, etc., the burial is recent, and we seem at a loss for their successors. On the other hand, of that mere talent that can almost pass muster as genius we have now-a-days a superfluity. Numbers are everywhere smothering the units ; the summits are lost sight of in the general heaving up of the common level. Every nation has too much brain-work of its own, it suffers too much of it to go to waste unnoticed or unheeded, to have leisure to bestow a thought on any but the most transcendant of its neighbours' productions. How could the Italians hope that their novels, however deserving, may be read or translated in a country like England, where the list of new novels in the national language rose in the course of last year (1885) to the prodigious number of four hundred and seventy ?

Hence, of the mass of books which have come out in Italy during this last score of years, only a few specimens of that lighter style of literature, which the Italians call *Letteratura amena*, a few *Bozzetti*, short tales or sketches, have found favour with the all-devouring generality of English readers; none so favourably received as the writings of Edmondo de Amicis, whose lifelike pictures of manners in large cities and unfrequented regions have appeared in neat English versions, and held their ground for more than one season in the London circulating libraries.

The Italians were, besides, hitherto in too grave and earnest a mood to care for what may be called the mere *cakes and ale* of literature. Their reading public is by no means extensive, and is circumscribed within the limits of their own territory. For five or even ten or twenty persons that may take pleasure in a book in England, we could find barely one in Italy itself; and Italian writers can only address themselves to their own public of 29,000,000; they may well envy, but not emulate, the success of their English *confrères*, whose language is the mother-tongue of 100,000,000 both within and without the limits of the British Empire. There is as yet, properly speaking, no literary centre in Italy, no sufficient intercourse of bibliographical intelligence up to very recent times. Milan knew but little of what came out in Rome; Florence cared even less for what Naples produced. There is no book-fair in Italy like that of Leipsic, no literary journal like the London 'Athenæum.' The 'Rassegna Settimanale' (Weekly Review), which aspired to assume its office, and which was edited by young men whose means

G 2

and liberality were on a par with their zeal for literature and their love of their country, had to be given up after two or three years, the subscribers never exceeding, if they ever reached, seven hundred and fifty. Publishers in Italy are not extravagant in their payment for *copy*, and it is but justice to say, that they can hardly afford to be generous, in a country where a new book, a volume of five hundred pages, is considered absurdly dear at five lire (4*s.*), its first edition being seldom expected to find five hundred purchasers. Italian writers are too often reduced to the condition of working for *love*, as very good people play whist. That Bentley or Hurst and Blackett pay, or ever paid, £3000 (75,000 lire) for a *rubbishing* lady's novel, or that a fortune can be made by supplying Mudie with *trash* at one guinea and a half for three volumes, or the railway stalls with their reprints at one shilling, is something that exceeds their comprehension. "In Italy, at all events," they say, "a novel does not fetch more than it is worth."

As an author in that country must too often accept honour for his sole payment, it is but natural that he should evince his preference for that style of composition which gives promise of more extensive usefulness and more enduring fame. Hence the cry

in Italy is for "solid" literature—for history, bio-
graphy, political science. Up to the middle of this
century it was the fashion for every Italian worth
his salt to be a patriot. After 1859 every patriot
became a politician. The country being made, the
next task was to govern it, or at least to enlighten,
exhort, oppose, or support those who undertook to
rule over it.

The journal became the ladder by which all
aspiring talent strove to make its way into public
life. Periodical publications, which were only 185
in 1836, and not quite twice that number thirty
years later, had risen to the number of 1425 in
December 1885. Of these 398 had a political
character; sixty-nine were "religious," and fifty-two
"*politico-religiosi*," i. e. clerical, interested in the cause
of the Pope's temporal sovereignty; the remainder
were literary, scientific, didactic, technical, etc. Most
of the reviews were fortnightly, like the French 'Revue
des Deux Mondes'; forty-seven were characterized as
humouristic papers, eight were illustrated.

In Italy the Press, whether it be a good or an
evil, has not yet reached the formidable proportions
it has developed in other democratized countries.
In France, at the close of 1885, the journals were

4359, of which 1540 appeared in Paris ; the political papers were numbered 1471, of which 962 were Republican, and 509 Monarchical.

Although, with few exceptions, Italian newspapers are worthless, their editors and writers are, in many instances, able men. Their knowledge is by no means vast, their language often uncouth or slovenly, more generally pompous and stilted ; but their judgment and tact are rarely at fault. Politics come to them, as it were, by intuition ; their statesmanship is mere guess-work, but their reasoning generally plausible, their eloquence now and then impassioned, stirring, and winning. Only in Italy journalism is seldom a permanent employment. The Italians seem not sufficiently to know and value the advantage of co-operation. They cannot manage to club together their means for a respectable leading newspaper. The half-penny broad-sheets are intended for a town or province, not for the country ; subservient to the views of a party or a *clique*, to the interests not of a class, but of an individual. The Press has no centre in Rome, though some of the journals of the capital, such as 'L'Opinione,' 'Fanfulla,' 'La Rassegna,' [1]

[1] Since the above was written 'La Rassegna' ceased to appear, in October, 1886.

etc., occupy an honourable position, and are backed
by a sufficient amount of talent and capital.
But none of these, nor the 'Nazione' of Florence,
nor the 'Perseveranza' of Milan, can be looked
upon as the organs of national opinion. The
paper which boasts the largest circulation (125,000
copies daily) is the 'Secolo,' a rabidly democratic
and anti-Catholic print of Milan ; and next to it,
it is believed, comes the 'Popolo Romano,' for very
good reasons 'an out-and-out champion of the Depretis Cabinet. None of these, it can be freely
asserted, circulate to any extent abroad, though
mention of them occasionally is made in Reuter's
telegrams. Some of the London clubs, which pride
themselves on gathering on their tables and shelves
the best specimens of the European Press, such as
the Athenæum Club, after taking up now one now
another of these Italian sheets, have ended by dis-
pensing with them all. And even the correspondents
of foreign, especially English, journals in Italy seem
seldom or never to have anything to say either of
the country or people, the interest for Italian political
or literary life having of late prodigiously cooled.
Telegrams about the Pope and Cardinals, about the
unburying of an ancient statue or fragment of a

statue, about the ravage of the sporadic cholera, and about the self-starving prodigies of Succi and Merlatti, is very nearly all that the 'Times' has day by day to tell us on the subject of living Italy. The Italians may console themselves with the saying that "a happy country has no history." The only literary journal known abroad and really deserving respect is the 'Nuova Antologia,' a fortnightly review or magazine, with contributions by Bonghi, Berti, Villari, and other writers of high distinction.

The fact is, that in Italy, as in France, newspaper writing is almost invariably a young man's trade. The editor's office is the ante-chamber to the House of Deputies, or even to the Minister's Cabinet. Every aspiring man sets up his own journal, works it all, or nearly all, by himself, and for his own ends, and drops it when his ends are attained, kicking down the ladder which helped him in his climbing. Hence the ephemeral character of all these periodical publications. We must not be surprised to hear, for instance, that 117 new journals were founded in Italy in one year, 1876; 151 in 1882; and 228 in 1883; very nearly an equal number of the old dying off year by year to make room for the new ones.

But if he has no chance for public life, the

journalist in Italy turns pamphleteer or essayist. Debarred from practice, he falls back upon theory. With the training of a penny-a-liner he ventures to grapple with the most arduous questions. A great part of the so-called serious political literature in Italy is essentially journalistic, superficial, and empirical.

But the man who has not sufficient ambition or self-confidence for public life, and does not aspire to the glory of swaying the destinies of his own country, is easily persuaded that, if he may not *act* history, he may at least *write* it. There is always a great deal of retrospective in all that appears in print in Italy. Italian writers are above all things chroniclers and antiquarians. Their mission seems to be rather to sweep the dust from the records of their ancestors' exploits than to show themselves their worthy descendants by emulating their deeds. History, it ought to be sufficiently plain and obvious, has accomplished its task in Italy. From Muratori downwards, the instinct of Italian annalists has been patriotic. They all worked with a purpose, and that was to illustrate Italy.

But of that work there has been almost enough. To Italian works on Italian history for the present

there might as well be an end. There could never
have been too many of those written by the men of
the last generation (Balbo, Cantù, La Farina, etc.),
because their object was to mature the great national
crisis. There could never be too many written by
the men actually engaged in the furtherance of the
crisis itself (Farini, Gualterio, etc.), because they, like
their ancestors of Macchiavello and Guicciardini's
time, acted and wrote by turns. But now the crisis
is over. Italy, let us repeat for the hundredth time,
is made. In Heaven's name, let us see what she is
made for! The world expects to know, not so
much what she has done as what she is going to do.
Now Italy should play a nobler part than that
of the *beccamorti* (undertaker or grave-digger) of old
Italy.

There is, with respect to this, decidedly too much
of a good thing. *Toujours de l'histoire* may be no
better than *toujour perdrix*. Besides the general
history of the country, there are endless publications
of mere municipal and provincial interest, illustrating
every nook and corner, unburying every monument,
deciphering every document, discussing every subject
connected with every locality in ancient, mediæval,
and modern Italy. One man alone, Muratori, might

be said to have done something to the purpose by his great folios of 'Rerum Italicarum Scriptores,' 'Antiquitates Italicæ,' etc., and by his twenty-two volumes of annals built upon them. But still, to eke out his vast achievements, deputations, associations, Royal and lately even Papal committees of *Storia Patria* are at work in every part of the country with a zeal which might as well be tempered by a little discretion. The same has been done about the history of Italian literature, where it might seem as if Tiraboschi and his continuators had left little undone on the subject, and where Corniani, Ugoni, Maffei, and other worthy scholars and critics, Italian and foreign (with Ginguené and Sismondi, and a number of Germans), had toiled to improve the original performance. Yet over and above all that we have new Italian literary histories by the score (those of Rovani, Ambrosoli, De Sanctis, San Filippo, Settembrini, Bartoli, etc.), besides the literary history compiled by a Society of Friends, and edited by Pasquale Villari; and besides what is done in every town and province to keep green the memory of local worthies by the celebration of anniversaries, centenaries, and tercentaries, by the publication of their lives and works, by the erection of statues, of memorial tablets, and tomb-stones, and by the dedication to them of streets and squares, which, with the childish fickleness of the French about their Place de la Concorde, are made to be re-christened at every new phase in the caprice of popular opinion.

All this is as it should be: well done, even if a little overdone. Any country which should neglect to do as much in honour of its great departed would incur universal blame; but history is not in itself literature. It only rises to the rank of a work of genius when it is taken in hand by such profound thinkers as Hume, by such acute critics as Gibbon, by such impartial champions of truth as Hallam or Ranke, by such wonderful word-painters as Carlyle.

There are historical works of great merit in Italy among those of the veteran scholars of the still-living generation. Michele Amari, whose eightieth birth-day has just been held in Italy almost as a national holiday, has lately brought out a greatly improved edition of his 'Sicilian Vesper,' and published the last volumes of the 'Mussulmans in Sicily.' Ercole Ricotti, the well-known author of the 'History of the Compagnie di Ventura' (free-lances of mediæval Italy), has been for years at work on a history of the monarchy of Savoy, published in six volumes, and not unlikely doom to oblivion the vast but ill-digested mass of good old Cibrario on the same subject. To the same category belong Emiliani Giudici's 'Storia dei Comuni Italiani,' the colossal works of Cantù on universal history, and some of the many monographs on the history of the largest cities, such as Celesia's 'Storia della Republica ed Università di Genova,' and 'La Congiura di Fiesco,' Peluso's 'Storia della Repubblica Milanese dal 1447 al 1450,' Molmenti's interesting 'Storia di Venezia nella vita privata,' and Bonacci's 'Storia di Perugia.'

Full justice, I think, has hardly been done to Gino Capponi's 'History of Florence,' a work to which the noble author consecrated forty years of his life (struggling against that same gloomy infirmity under which the American Prescott was labouring), yet which is now comparatively put aside, partly because, while its publication was impatiently looked forward to, other writers, chiefly foreign (Napier, Trollope, Reumont, Thiers, etc.), striving to test the truth of the subject by the light of newly-dis-covered documents, and stealing a march upon him, planned, and some of them carried on the works to a termination, but more especially because Capponi, who, as a historian, cared for truth even more than for his country, disdained to truckle to the ultra-democratic passions and prejudices now cherished by many of his contemporaries, and painted the liberty of the Florentine Republic as it really was, *i. e.* as a suicidal frenzy which, though it called forth such energies as made the city of the Arno for above two centuries the fountain-head of the art and science of the whole world, and the centre of its active life, was yet sure to lead, first to the splendid enslavement, then to the rapid decline and tragic end of that unruly community.

Hardly less important than the historical are some of the biographical publications of the Italy of the present day. The studies of Pasquale Villari on Savonarola; those of the same author, and of Oreste Tommasini, on Macchiavello; those of Domenico Berti on Giordano Bruno, Tommaso Campanella, Giovanni Valdes, Copernicus, Galileo, etc., all touch on subjects on which the learned, especially of England and Germany, have worked with good will hand-in-hand with their Italian contemporaries. Biographical works of another kind have been suggested by friendship, as Bonghi's ' Life of Valentino Pasini,' Tullo Massarani's ' Life of Luigi Tenca '; or by filial affection, like the ' Memorie di Giuseppe Pasolini,' or the 'Memorie di un Editore' (Barbèra). A work of higher pretensions as to style is Bonfadini's 'Mezzo Secolo di Patriottismo,' chiefly relating the sufferings of the prisoners of Spielberg and other State fortresses, of those who had not themselves already told their own tale, and especially of the heroic 'Federigo Confalonieri.'

The Italian historians of the present day are for the most part painstaking and diligent in their researches for such information as can throw the best light on the subject engaging their attention ; but they are not unfrequently deficient in that encyclopædical knowledge, which might enable them to form a just estimate of the importance of their particular subject in the general history of mankind. They lack the elements of comparison. Not many of them are linguists, not many travel ; their views are necessarily one-sided, their range of thought cramped and limited ; they are also too patriotic, too partial, too easily persuaded that *toute vérité, n'est pas bonne à dire.* Men of the strict conscientiousness of Hallam or Ranke are very rare among them. Nor are there among modern Italian historians many venturing upon foreign subjects. The last was Botta's 'History of the War of Independence of the United States of

America,' now an old book; and there is an announce-
ment of a 'Storia della Conquista Inglese delle Indie,'
by Clemente Corte, a member of the Italian Senate.

Italy, on the contrary, is the subject on which
foreigners always took an almost patriotic interest.
Niebuhr, Bunsen, Leo, Ranke, Mommsen, Gregorovius, with other Germans, have made themselves at
home in the southern land, with the main if not the
only object of studying and illustrating its glorious
past. They bring with them the energies, the patience,
and industry to which the steady discipline of their
own schools have accustomed them; the deep methods
of thought by which the wide sphere of their knowledge empowers them to lay down facts and generalize
upon them, to draw inferences from obvious premises,
and to refer effects to the remotest causes.

It is greatly to the credit of the Italians that they
fairly acknowledge their own inferiority to these illustrious aliens, and neither show nor feel any mean
jealousy of them. They look up to them, to the
above-named, as well as to Schiff, Moleschott, and to
the late lamented Hillebrand, as their teachers in
the various branches of learning in which they excel.
They tempt them by every demonstration of honour,
by the offer of stipends exceeding the ordinary

salaries of their own professors, by the witchery of their coaxing manners, which would remain as the peculiar charm of the Italian race, were even all their other more solid qualities lost, tempt them, I say, to take up their permanent abode under their bright southern sky, and to forget the honoured *vaterland* among the seductions of their adopted country.

It is a reproduction of the phenomenon of the Italy of the Renaissance, when Petrarch, Boccaccio, and the men of the Medici Court won by their loving hospitality the hearts of the Greek scholars, fugitives from the inroads of the Turks, took them to their bosoms (grizzly bears as some of them were), and, by becoming their pupils, re-opened in their own new Italy the spring of that ancient classical lore which the trampling of the northern invaders and the austerity of religious intolerance had trodden down and dried up.

CHAPTER. V.

SCIENCE AND ART.

Italian Science—Character of the Italian Mind—Italy's Part in the Advancement of Science—Italian Scientific Men—Past and Present—Italian Art—Academies—Their Influence—Causes of Decline in Painting—Better chances for Sculpture—Realism in Art—The Cavour Monument—The Italians charged with Vandalism.

THERE is one point on which the judgment of foreign critics, with respect to the intellectual faculties of the Italians, is materially at variance with the opinion the Italians entertain of themselves. Foreigners for the most part allow the gift of brightness to the Italian mind; but they grudge it the merit of solidity. "Larks and swifts," they say, "may best flutter in the glare of a southern sun; but the pathetic nightingale loves to hide in the deepest forest shade, and the brooding owl delights in the coolness of a nightly northern temperature."

On the other hand, the Italians are apt to claim more than their share of the achievements of man-

kind in every branch of learning—in the most severe
and positive, as well as in the lightest and most
genial pursuits. Their position as the centre of
light in the ancient world, they think, enabled them
to take the initiative in science as well as in art.
Italy was the land of the *Renaissance*, the cradle of
thought. It was natural, whether or not it was
always just, that she who struck out the first path
should have the merit of having also laid open the
broadest thoroughfare. Centuries of prostration have
not rooted this fond conceit out of Italian hearts.
It was by them, the Italians contend, that the all-
important facts in science were revealed. That what
they began other people accomplished, they cannot
be unwilling to admit. But, as in the discovery
of America, so in every branch of knowledge, they
insist, there has almost invariably been a case of
sic vos non vobis. Italians have shown the way, they
have given their names to new worlds, but they have
never known how to turn them to their own
advantage.

But this, their neighbours argue, is in the very
nature of things; it is the result of circumstances.
The honour of a discovery is due, not so much to
the man who by chance or inspiration hits on a new

fact, as to him who manages to work it out, to improve upon it, till he applies it to some available practical purpose.

To take an instance from olden times : of that greatest step in the science of physiology, the discovery of the circulation of the blood, the Italians would fain take the credit on themselves, simply on the fact that Harvey studied at Padua, under Fabrizio d'Acquapendente, whose remarks on the valvular structure of the veins (according to Harvey's own statement) suggested the first idea which the great English disciple carried on to such splendid results. No doubt Padua was then at the head of medical science. No doubt Fabrizio himself, and the illustrious triumvirate who preceded him (Fallopius, Eustachius, and Vesalius), and no doubt Andrea Cesalpino also, and Fra Paolo Sarpi, may have had a glimmering of the truth. But the fate of Sarpi himself proved what chance truth might have in the Italy of Pius V., and of his truculent Catholic reaction ; while Harvey had the good fortune of carrying such knowledge as he had picked up in that slough of despond that an Italian University was soon to become, to a country fanned by the wholesale breezes of Protestant freedom, a freedom which, whatever it may have done for man's welfare in another world, had certainly removed all limits to the spread of man's knowledge of the things of this earthly abode. It is questionable whether any of the above-named Italian doctors, or all of them, would have had the skill and patience wherewith the brave Englishman built up his theory (1628), or the constancy with which he withstood the clamorous opposition raised against him, even in England, by "the obstinate foolish old school." [1] But in Italy he would, besides, have had to confront all the enmity of the priests— of those priests who, only five years later (1633), were strong enough to convince poor Galileo against his will.

It is full time, I think, for all nations to divest themselves of mean jealousies and petty vanities. Genius and learning are of all ages and countries, the common heritage of all the tribes of mankind. It is not what a nation contributed to the stores of knowledge in olden times that matters much (else the palm might perhaps be due to Egypt and Greece), but the all-important is what every country brings

[1] " La superstizïon del Ver nemica,
E l'ostinata folle scuola antica."
Parini, *L'Innes'o del Vaiuolo.*

to the common treasure day by day; and, judged
by that standard, I am afraid that Italy, in her
neighbours' estimation, is still far from making up
for the time she has lost since the days of Harvey and
Galileo.   There is now no inquisition in Italy.   The
Pope has ceased to be a prince or an adviser and abettor of princes ; but he is still a priest ; and what becomes
of the science of a man who allows a priest to have
a hold on his conscience ?   The conciliation of scientific
with religious truth is the task at which even Pro-
testantism has for three centuries been labouring in
vain.   In England professors like Huxley, and statesmen like Gladstone, are still in the pages of the
Nineteenth Century fighting that battle which will
probably be a drawn game to the end of time.   But
among the Latin races in Roman Catholic countries,
at least in revolutionized France, the problem has
admitted of an easy solution.   The man of science
has either renounced all belief, or he simply *professes*,
i. e. *pretends* to believe.   In Italy, as yet not so
utterly lost to all faith as France is, the battle is
fought, but not in the open field, not with fair loyal
weapons.   Blind believers and blank unbelievers in
that country are equally afraid to speak out, actually
loth to make up their minds.   " What is the use of

controversy?" the Italians think. "Let science go its own way, and let God take care of His truth! Man should go to school to learn, and to Church to pray—free as to going to Church, though bound by law to go to school. His own instinct must determine his choice between his teacher and his confessor."

I have already shown how in their schools and high schools the Italians have come to what they think a plausible, but other nations consider an impracticable, compromise. They have to contend with what is an almost insurmountable difficulty in all countries, but especially in those freshly emancipated from political and ecclesiastical thraldom; for sudden enfranchisement must inevitably for a time carry liberty to the extremes of licence.

But that is not the only obstacle to the progress of Italian science. The Italian universities, as I also said, are too numerous, too small, too poor, to have either the sufficiency of material means or the efficiency of method and discipline, the division of labour, and the communion of thought necessary to pursue scientific inquiry to its ultimate results of theoretical and practical development. And there is, therefore, not enough of that stern earnestness of purpose, of that keen intensity of application, which in other countries arises from emulation and competition. The want of a great centre, which I have noticed as damaging to the interests of literature, equally or more strongly stands in the way of the advancement of science. Every man in Italy is apt to keep to the little circle of his own town and province, content, like Cæsar, to be first in an Alpine village rather than second in Rome; and the worst is that he is often as easily held to be the first in his immediate neighbours' estimation as he is in his own. Men in Italy have little opportunity of weighing and valuing one another. There is not enough of that intercourse, of that rubbing together, as it were, which makes even stones strike light-sparks.

Italy, it is felt, is not intellectually as united a country as she is politically. With the hope of counteracting this acknowledged evil of isolation, Congresses, or meetings of the *Scienziati* or *Savants*, from all parts of the peninsula, are held every year in some of the large cities, both general and special meetings, analogous to those of the British Association. These not only began several years before the emancipation of the peninsula, but in some measure preluded, and indeed were partly instrumental to it. Of late, also, under the auspices of

King Humbert, and by the exertions of the universally lamented Quintino Sella, the famous Academy dei Lincei has been revived in Rome, its original residence, and is intended to perform the functions of the French Institute, and of the English Royal Society.

The re-opening of this time-honoured scientific association on the 16th December, 1884, after a long period of silence and obscurity, will not do away with the existing Istituto Lombardo of Milan, the Accademia delle Scienze in Turin and Naples, the many Istituti Superiori of Florence, etc. The purpose is to give all such local institutions a rallying point and a head; but whether such an object be attainable, and to what extent, seems doubtful; for concentration of power is not much in the habits and instincts, indeed, not in the nature of the Italian people. No city in Italy, and not even the Eternal City, will ever have the absorbing attraction which London and Paris exercise over England and France; nor would perhaps too great a centralization be in all respects desirable; for Italy, like Germany, aspires to combine unity with variety, and it is well that it should be so within all practicable limits. But for what concerns science, there is no doubt that the existence of so many rival establishments must be a hindrance to general progress. Poetry and all light literature may spring from individual inspiration; but positive knowledge relies on extensive culture and aggregate effort. Individually, and while relying on his own unaided resources, there is hardly any task an Italian brain has not at all ages proved to be equal to. There have been giants in that country in olden times (Dante, Petrarch, Marsilio Ficino, Pico della Mirandola, and more than I need mention), phenomena of men whose heads carried all the knowledge at which the world had then arrived; and traces of the same powers have constantly shown themselves even throughout the period of Italy's most calamitous times. The Italian may lack the will, but seldom the aptitude for hard work, seldom that " power of taking pains," which, in the opinion of a great thinker, is the main character of true genius. Who ever did more for the compilation of historical or literary documents than Muratori, Tiraboschi, or Angelo Mai? or where was there a linguist of more extensive requirements than Mezzofanti? or what English librarian did more for the British Museum than Antonio Panizzi? or for that matter, and looking to the present generation, where are there more indefatigable labourers in the field of knowledge than Cesare Cantù or Ruggero Bonghi? or, to do justice even to the *Dii Minores*, than Angelo de Gubernatis, Michele Lessona, Girolamo Boccardo?

Unwearied energies, minute diligence, heroic endurance are not uncommon qualities of the Italian mind ; and what is more remarkable, they are found not unfrequently in the most eminent degree in those soft paradisical climates of the south where, for want of proper training, the race appears more lax and unnerved. It is from Naples, that overgrown town which, with its immediate territory, must in many respects be allowed to be the very sink of corruption and the plague-spot of Italy—it is from Naples, I say, that some of the most daring and robust thinkers have astonished the world.

There have been in the very worst times good workers in Italy. From the days of Galileo to those of Piazzi, Donati, and Secchi there have been astronomers. From Vico, Genovesi, Beccaria, Filangieri, to Romagnosi, Rosmini, Gioberti, there have been theoretical and practical philosophers. In natural science, in political economy, in moral philosophy, the tradition of Italian eminence has been faithfully maintained and transmitted. New thinkers have ever been ready to fill the places vacated by death. Nor are those places left empty in the living generation. The Lincei Academy, whose complete number in Italy itself should be one hundred, has hitherto not been carried beyond seventy-nine. Of these a score or so might be named, thoroughly known and honoured, both in and out of Italy, to the full extent of their worth. And there are even some whose reputation is more extensively and more solidly established abroad than at home, men who, owing either to professional jealousy, or more probably to the narrow sphere in which they moved all their lives, have never had their merits duly acknowledged in their own country, till, like opera singers, actors, or dancers, they have gone back to it after some absence with the prestige of their fame established by success in foreign lands. So far is Italy still from being intellectually one and the same country.

What has hitherto been said about science applies with even greater force to art. For the academies of painting and sculpture outnumber the schools of law and physic, and one would say that the mere fact that Italy is bringing up many artists would be sufficient to justify her titles to the appellation of

the Land of Art; whereas such a distinction should
be awarded, not to the workers' number, but to the
excellence of their work, and the honour in which it
is held. Everything in Italy seems contrived to
foster mediocrity; nothing to reward the toil which
alone can lead to the attainment of superior capacity.

In the ages of divided Italy one heard very naturally of Tuscan and Roman, Lombard, Venetian, and
other provincial art schools. But after the unifica-
tion of the country one would say that new schools
shoot up in every town or borough. Exhibitions are
opened in every insignificant locality, at the same
time that in Rome, in the Via Nazionale, an edifice
has been reared in rather questionable artistic taste,
meant for the palace or temple of national art. But
alas! what art? Miles of painted canvas, tons of
carved marble, most of it unsold or unsaleable ware,
stock every spring or autumn market throughout the
country. Thanks to the liberality of national or
municipal institutions, it costs little or nothing to
bring up a painter or sculptor; it costs even less than
to fit out a lawyer or physician. The misfortune is,
that if there is little bread for the professional man
who attends to the necessities of life, there is even
less, indeed there too often is none, for the artist who

only ministers to its luxuries. A man who paints because he must eat cannot care much about the style of excellence at which his work should aim. What can be soonest done and soonest sold is for him the *ne plus ultra*. It is not his own judgment, it is not the cultivated taste of the few that he can allow himself to consult. He must pander to the common fashion, to the fickle caprice of the multitude, and he cannot even look for his reward to the candid opinion of fair critics ; for praise in the most fulsome, most absurdly transcendent style is, as a rule, bestowed by the press indiscriminately on the veriest daubs ; the writer, either from personal friendship, from local patriotism, or from mistaken goodnature, so recklessly lavishing his superlatives where they are least deserved, as to be at a loss for words to do justice to real merit, even if he had the taste and judgment necessary to discover and appreciate it.

There are, no doubt, artists of considerable merit in the Italy of the present generation. Some of them come up burning with that zeal and enthusiasm which the instinct of the beautiful, and which the achievements of the great masters in the galleries cannot fail to kindle in every generous breast. Correggio's brave

word, "I too am a painter," is the first occurring to
every puny young dauber's conceit. But what comes
of it? For the first and second season one hears of some
ambitious youth whose early essays are proclaimed as
works of marvellous promise by the professors, many
of whom, not being themselves swans, are rather apt
to over-value their own brood of goslings. Ussi's
'Cacciata del Duca d'Atene,' for instance, a work of
undoubted talent, as well as of large dimensions,
excited the highest expectation as to the opening
career of a wonder-working young artist. But what
of it? That picture appeared at the first exhibition
of free Florence in 1861, and was subsequently re-
produced at almost every other world's show throughout Europe. But what followed? From that year
to the present what has anywhere been seen or heard
of Ussi? There was, we were told, another picture by
the same hand, 'Bianca Cappello,' which he destroyed,
and some sketches, 'Impressioni' of travels in the
East, are also mentioned; but that apparently is all
the world may expect to have out of six-and-twenty
years of a really great painter's life.

There are other artists' names celebrated in Italy,
and several enjoying not a little renown abroad.
In the midst of a vast farrago of rubbish which

chills your blood with dismay, or makes it boil
with indignation, as you walk along the walls of an
academical exhibition (at some of which, for greater
outrage, the crude performances of the present day
are hung by the side, or at least in sight of the
highly-finished masterpieces of former ages), you
come now and then upon some works of higher
pretensions, and not without claims to originality.
What is most striking in many of them is the
preference given by the artists, or possibly by their
customers (when they find any), to gloomy and dismal
subjects, which may perhaps reveal the prevailing
tendency of the bilious southern temperament.
What occurs frequently in the Italian historical
pictures, illustrating national episodes, and prompted
by patriotic instincts, are such scenes as ' Ezzelino
da Romano wounded and dying in captivity,' ' Savonarola at the death-bed of Lorenzo de' Medici,'
' Michael Angelo gazing at the dead face of Vittoria
Colonna,' ' Pietro Micca blowing up himself and his
French enemies in the vault underneath a Turin
bastion,' ' The Dying Columbus bidding his son to
bury his gyves with him in his grave,' and the
like. Works, some of them of almost classical value,
there are, yet hardly any of them find a purchaser,

unless it be the king out of his private purse, or the artist's own native city, the academy which nurtured him, or some other public corporation straining its little resources to perform an act, half of patronizing munificence, half of sheer charity.

With the exception of the ancient masters, the Italians have seldom been first-rate portrait or landscape painters. Their best support in ancient time was the Church ; and of 'Madonnas,' 'Ecce Homos,' and 'Holy Families,' the present age is rather bent on stripping than enriching the sacred buildings. The priest is now too poor a patron of art, and of "undraped" Venuses, France has for many years claimed the unenviable monopoly. High art in Italy, it seems taken for granted, can only deal with historical subjects; and of those taken from Italian annals, it is naturally supposed that English lords or Russian Boyards (the representatives of tourist wealth and patronage) would understand little and care even less.

Que faire ? Il faut vivre ! And, after a few feeble attempts, the most ambitious artist gives up the game, and condescends, as a mere drudge, to supply prints and curiosity shops with some sketches, articles *de genre*, etc., mere nick-nacks of art, which cost little trouble and yield prompt returns.   Ussi, for instance, won recently very high praise, and, let us hope, also solid remuneration, by his drawings intended as illustrations to the book on ' Morocco ' of De Amicis.

It is owing to all these circumstances that we hear throughout Europe loud clamour about the decline or decay of Italian art, and of the wretched figure Italy plays in that respect at any of the universal exhibitions by the side not only of the great nations, France, Germany, and England, but also of smaller communities, especially of Belgium, Holland, and Switzerland. Italian artists are received with somewhat greater favour at the Paris Salon, probably owing to the preference they have evinced, as imitators, to French rather than to other Transalpine models.

It is otherwise with sculpture.   The Hyde Park Exhibition of 1851 struck its million visitors with wonder at the talent of some Milanese artists, whose marbles filled a " court " in the Austrian department, at the door of which, doing duty as sentry, stood the grim effigy of old Marshal Radezky.   It was a revelation to untravelled Europe of what was going on unsuspected in Italy in the way of sculptural work.   The names of Marchesi, Monti, Vela, etc., hitherto only known to foreign tourists, became ex-

tensively famous; at the next show in South Kensington (1862), the world became familiar with the
works of Finelli, Tantardini, Dupré, Monteverde,
Pampaloni, etc., till it began to be understood that
Italy could muster a sufficient number of worthy
pupils of Bartolini and Tenerani—the men of the last
generation, who in their turn had been perpetuating
the traditions of Canova and Thorwaldsen.

The reason why these two main branches of art,
painting and her sister sculpture, meet in Italy with
such different success may be easily pointed out.
The hand of the Italian artist, it seems, has not yet
forgot its cunning. It is rather the head or heart
that is at fault. Enough, and more than enough,
is done in that country to bring up as cultivators
of art thinking and feeling human beings; but
the result is, too generally, to produce mere limning
and carving machines. The best endowed Italian
academies of art can boast a whole staff of able professors appointed to lecture in their halls on history,
on æsthetics, on perspective, on harmony of colours,
on every branch of knowledge calculated to elevate
the students' thoughts, to fire their imagination, to
inspire them with the instinct, not only of what is
physically, but also of what is mentally and morally

beautiful. The intention evidently is to look upon all the resources of poetry and philosophy as the proper dowry and heritage of art.

Much of what the teacher would and could impart, however, is lost upon the idle disposition of the pupils. We have seen that there is no very hard work among the students of an Italian university, where, however, there is still some show of examination for degrees to call the candidate to account for the employment of his time. But no such restraint, feeble as it is, is put upon the apprentices at an artistic academy. The young painter is taken, like a horse, to the waters of knowledge. It is for him to drink to the extent of his thirst. If there is anything in him like a spark of genius, it will be seen in the specimens he will bring to the yearly exhibition.

What comes of this? A certain amount of plastic instinct, of discriminating taste, and imitative skill is seldom absent in a southern organization. Such phenomena as a young goatherd with the fingers of a Giotto, or two plain girls with the ears and the touch of the sisters Milanollo (mere children, whose genius seems to spring up full-grown almost before the hands can reach the easel or the piano), are not less common in Italy than they formerly were, or than they are now in any other land where the sun shines. But an Italian youth and his trainer are too apt to think that in the way of art all is best left to mere nature. They are too much convinced, as a well-known poet was, that "your true genius never reads."

"There is a tree!" says the teacher. "Yonder a hut, the outlines of a hill, a dairy-maid and cow, anything in nature that may strike your fancy. Here you have the *gesso*, the *nudo* (the plaster-cast, the naked model), the Great Master's work, all before you. You have your chalk, your colours, your brushes, your canvas, your clay, your marble, all the tools of your craft near at hand. Go and reproduce what you see."

And the learner goes and does what he is bidden. The mere mechanical skill of an Italian artist is so thorough, that one may buy in Florence or Naples the copy of a Raphael, a Titian, a Guido, a Holbein, or a Velasquez, which only the most consummate *connoisseur* will be able to distinguish from the original. So much for the mere hand. But what about the head? You have made a good copyist; but where is your artist? Ambition will prompt a clever youth to high art, but it will be an attempt to fly with ostrich wings. He will be on the look-out for an historical subject; but what does he know about history? In what stores of his mind can he find the ideal of his hero's character? What inspiration can suggest the true expression of his heroine's countenance? What did Marochetti make out of his equestrian statue of Richard Cœur de Lion? Simply an armed youth on a caparisoned steed. What could he make out of a Sappho? Marochetti, an Italian by birth, was brought up in Paris. He was an accomplished academician, a polished gentleman; but all his thinking and feeling faculties had never gone through a proper development. He was a mere materialist in art, and so are most, both of his French and Italian contemporaries; unable to feel that they must bring souls as well as bodies, meaning as well as form or colour, out of their canvas or marble.

Such a deficiency in the studies which ought to be considered indispensable auxiliaries to the attainment of excellence in the artist's craft, such disregard of character and costume, such liability to fall into all kinds of incongruity and anachronism, are faults, it is true, often found in the old masters, though seldom in the very great; but their faults are not their merits. *Ce n'est pas ce qu'ils ont fait de mieux.*

And there is no reason why what was tolerated in them should be allowed to men who are to suit the more fastidious taste of a more enlightened age. Yet this same overweening trust in mere natural gifts, this blind disregard of all but the strictly technical acquirements, run through every artistical pursuit in Italy. You have there musical composers, like Rossini, who "don't care a straw" to what nonsense in the *Libretto* they wed their heavenly melodies. You have singers like Rubini, angels as to their voices, but "mere sticks" on the stage as actors.

Matters are beginning to mend in Italy at the present day. That conception is of as great importance as execution, that the brain must have its part as well as the eye, that a picture must appeal to the understanding as well as to the senses, are notions to which Italian artists are gradually, though still somewhat reluctantly, won over. All theory of art is to many of them "mere pedantry." "Why should they need more school learning," they ask, "than what sufficed Perugino, Carlo Dolci, or Correggio ?"

It is evident that this lack of intellectual culture must interfere with the task of the painter more disastrously than with that of the sculptor. For this latter works on simpler material : he deals with his subject more abstractedly, needs look less to mere accessories, and relies for effect on form more easily reducible to the exact measurement of rule and compass. The mere stone-cutter takes upon himself no little part of the sculptor's work; and in some instances he ought to come in for a larger share of the gain and praise awarded to his foreign, and especially, if report is correct, to his American employer, often a mere amateur who covets fame as an artist. Italy has, besides, almost the monopoly of fine marbles, and the demand for the carver's work is not limited to statues or busts for the galleries, but extends to a large variety of monumental and ornamental achievements, associating it with architecture in every phase of public and private life, and suiting it to the style of southern house-building and gardening.

But although the sculptor's trade is more brisk and better paid, his intellectual development does not rise much above that of his brother artist, the painter. In both cases, as indeed in everything else, one can perceive the effect of all-pervading French influence. Italian art, like Italian literature, is now-a-days attempting to reconcile the realism of the present with the idealism of the last generation, a very arduous and by no means profitable undertaking.

The deplorable effects of this merely material training of artists may be seen in the latter works of Dupré, a sculptor lately deceased, and to whose memory very high honours have been paid this very summer of 1886. Giovanni Dupré, a native of Siena, brought up by his father in his trade of a wood-carver, set up in Florence later in life as a worker in marble, and soon displayed the talent of a self-made man. By his ' Abel,' by his ' Cain,' and other youthful productions, by his ' Sappho,' his ' Giotto,' and other works in maturer age, he won a fair name, and placed himself at the head of his calling to such an extent, that when a monument to Cavour had to be erected in Turin, he had little difficulty in distancing all his competitors.

The Cavour monument was finished and inaugurated in the summer of 1873. It is a group of ten colossal figures, in the centre of which sits a fat Cavour with a still fatter Italy, the latter kneeling and resting her ample bosom on the hero's knees; all the figures of the group as little encumbered with drapery as the hottest sun of an Italian August may make it desirable : Cavour simply wrapped in a loose sheet, Italy bare to her hips and a little further down ; the main figures hardly more decent than the meaningless allegorical nymphs sprawling around them. The great fame of the artist struck dumb the spectators at the unveiling of the group, at which the artist was well known to have worked for ten years. But the impression that it was an egregious failure, an outrage both to judgment and taste, was general, and in spite of the high finish of the whole workmanship, no one should be surprised if the fate of the Cavour monument in Turin were ultimately to be the same as that which, in obedience to the irresistible outcry of public opinion, befel the Wellington statue at Hyde Park corner.

No doubt Cavour was fat, and had by no means classical features ; but there was a great heart as well as a great brain in him, and it was the artist's duty either to find it in him or to give it to him in the expression of the countenance, and in the attitude of the figure. There is no mistaking the great man's character, no overlooking his genius, in the many excellent, however perishable, photographs that we have of him, yet which the sculptor failed to transfer to his everlasting marble.

But even admitting that the creative powers of Italian genius are for a season dormant, it does not seem credible that all the sense of the beautiful should at once have died off in what was till yesterday the land of taste. Anxious as I am to divest myself of all partiality to my countrymen, I certainly cannot join the insane outcry raised of late by foreign visitors against "Italian Vandalism." The veneration of the Italians for their treasures of art and antiquity is carried to the extremes of superstitious worship. The zeal with which excavations are pursued in Rome, at Pompeii, and elsewhere, under the present rulers, exceeds anything ever evinced by Pope or Bourbon, even when acting under the auspices of munificent French Imperialism. Never has aught been done with more diligence or judgment, never with wiser thrift and management, never also with more signal results than those diggings at Rome of the present day. And this is not denied. The charge is not of inactivity, but of barbaric demolition, or of more fatal, careless and senseless, shabby or tawdry restoration.

Foreign critics in their clamour seem to overlook

several important facts. In the first place, they appear to forget that man's works are not imperishable. The whole of Italy is a museum; the monuments of the past are by thousands, many of them crumbling to dust. Were all the resources of Italy (even with the most liberal subventions of Europe, if indeed the very men who so loudly claim these national monuments as the common heritage of civilized mankind would contribute a farthing for their preservation), were all the world's resources devoted to the sole purpose of staying incessant decay, time would still have its victory. The vastness of the repairs required, the difficulty and the cost of carrying them out, and the inadequacy of the forthcoming funds, however large, would still drive the restorers to shifts to which "their poverty, though not their will or their taste, would consent." What could be done, for instance, when the alternative lies between patching up anyhow a church or a palace in Venice (and it turns out now [1] that the repairs have been done with the utmost care and reverence), and suffering it to totter on the wooden piles eternally rotting underneath? To do nothing would no doubt have been

[1] See the letters from Venice in the 'Times' of this August, 1886.

the easiest. And that is what has been done by former generations, by whom perhaps better results might have been obtainable had they not disregarded the golden maxim about "a stitch in time."

Again, foreign censors should consider that "*Il faut vivre*," "*Il faut être de son temps*," that the Italians must live, and be the men of the present. That there should be *vaporetti*, or steamboat-omnibuses, in the Canal Grande, from the station to the Piazzetta, as there were *barconi*, or big row-boat-omnibuses in Austrian times, may seem a great outrage. But what would you have? The gondola, though smoothly gliding, was too slow. The gondolier, though a picturesque and musical, witty and pleasant-spoken rogue, was often too disreputable. His "floating coffin," like Figaro's shop, too readily lent itself to amorous intrigues, lawful or unlawful.

Neither Italy nor any country can stick for ever to what no longer answers the exigencies of modern travel. The *barcone* was contrived for safety and decency, the *vaporetto* for speed. It is the inexorable law of progress. Even with the recent appliances of railway, and translagoonar bridge, poor Venice, the Venice of the Bucentaur and of the Doge, wedding the sea, has now a hard struggle for existence. But without them she would long since have been, as her lover, Byron, wished,[1] "whelmed beneath the waves."

The same with Rome. It was a fatal necessity for the Italians to claim their ancient capital. But it was no easy task for a living nation to make its bed in a cemetery. They had to tread upon the tombstones, and almost on the very bones of half-buried generations; to find room for themselves among the ruins of the Ancient and Mediæval, the Christian and Pagan world. A multitude of 324,649 inhabitants had in 1884 to find shelter where in 1870 there were only 221,000, with an average yearly influx of 5600 newcomers. The Italians did all in their power. They did not all find their abode in the city; they built themselves suburbs. They could not widen the old streets; they opened new thoroughfares. Not to interfere with old Rome, they laid out the plans of many new Romes. But nothing could equal their forbearance. Between Porta del Popolo and the Capitol, and from the Pincio to the Vatican, and especially in the dear English *Ghetto*, there is hardly

---

[1] " Better be whelmed beneath the waves, and shun,
    Even in destruction's depth, her foreign foes,
    From whom submission wrings an infamous repose."
                        'Childe Harold,' Canto iv. st. xiii.

any perceptible change, unless it be the removal of those *Immondezzai*, or dirt heaps, which were the delight of the lover of the picturesque in the Papal city. That city has hardly been touched. The country around it lies in all its former silence and squalor, though works are beginning for that drainage which is to give health and fertility to the region, and for that embankment of the Tiber which is to save the lowest quarters of the town from those periodical inundations with which Papal rule had for centuries blessed them.

All has not been wisely, not elegantly, or artistically done, no doubt. Blocks of unseemly, staring, and in many cases flimsy buildings have been run up in the outskirts, round *Piazza di Termini*, in the deserts round the Lateran, in the cut-throat haunts of the *Prati di Castello*. They are such structures as great hurry, poverty, and greedy speculation have to provide for a too rapid spread of the population in every growing town. But among many common-place rows in Rome one sees some very fine and even grand buildings, not in bad taste though modern, and certainly not in keeping with the shabby and lurid appearance of the immense majority of the old Roman dwellings. But the centre remains as it was,

Papal, priestly, monastic, and outwardly at least without a shadow of taste ; and no one can say how long it may continue so, how long the past will stand in the way of the present and future. What would the grumblers have ? Did they expect the capital of a new nation could for ever remain the old heaps of rubbish and curiosity shops the priests had made it ? Italian Rome must live, and "let the dead past bury its dead." [1] But meanwhile, that the Italians have behaved in Rome as Alaric's Goths or Genseric's Vandals did, is an assertion which might well be allowed to embittered fanatic Ultramontanes, which might be echoed by the set of Tom-noddies, idle English club men, bewigged German professors, and *femmes incomprises*, which make up the rank and file of the idle Roman army of tourists, but which one could hardly hear without regret when spoken by unprejudiced lovers of art, antiquity, and—truth.

I am sorry to have to allude to losses of far graver nature ; that of objects of art or antiquity which the country has lately suffered from the breach of trust of the men in charge of Italian museums, galleries, etc. In the only two provincial cities I had occasion to visit

---

[1] "Let the dead past bury its dead."
Longfellow, 'A Psalm of Life.'

very valuable ancient MSS. were missing, in all probability stolen from the royal libraries, with the connivance of faithless attendants, some of whom had the very best characters for many years' honourable service, but who, nevertheless, were awaiting their trial with little hope of clearing themselves. In the new Victor Emmanuel Library, in the former Collegio Romano, if we may believe the Roman papers, as many as one hundred and twenty of such treasures have also mysteriously disappeared. Similar occurrences of pictures stolen from galleries or churches, with the probable complicity of the care-takers (as of one of the Raphael's from the artist's native place, lately mentioned in the papers), are not as unfrequent as one would wish. The appointment of new and in many cases hard-tried officials, their wretchedly low wages, and the large bribes held out by foreign tourists, or by their dishonest agents, easily explain such incidents; but do not make them by any means less deplorable or disgraceful.

CHAPTER VI.

EDUCATION.

Instruction *v.* Education—Physical Training—Condition of the Lower Classes—Starvation or Emigration—Public and Private Charity—The Upper Classes—Landowners and Land-labourers —Necessity for a Manly Education—Day and Boarding Schools —Italian Manly Exercises—Ancient and Modern—Enervating and Corrupting Home Influences—Education of Women— Symptoms of Improvement.

I NEED hardly refer to the authority of Alfieri's well-known saying about the excellence of the "Plant Man" in Italy, to assert that there are in the native race of that country all the physical, mental, and moral elements needful to constitute a great nation. It all depends on the way her rulers go to work about the development of those elements. The question is whether the culture is as provident as the soil is bountiful; whether the political, social, and moral institutions are calculated to exercise a beneficent or pernicious influence.

I have in some of the foregoing chapters pointed

out what seems to me the main fault in the civil
organization of the new Italian kingdom. I have
exposed the evil tendencies of such literary activity
as these latter years have brought to light. I have
insisted especially on the defectiveness of the scholastic establishments, proving how they do not sufficiently, do not at all, answer their avowed purpose;
how they merely attend to instruction, while the
pressing demand is for education. On this latter
subject there is more to be said. The Italian race
needs strengthening. The most immediate want is
physical training. The first thing to be considered
is their diet. The Southern climate is made to bear
the blame of a multitude of sins. Among them
the charge is laid upon it that the people are too
wretchedly fed. And yet it would be easy to prove
that among the lower orders, and especially among
the labouring peasantry, it is not by any means a
good appetite or a better digestion that is at fault;
that it is not from choice that they live almost
exclusively on *maccaroni*, or *polenta;* that in their
squalid hovels all over the country many a large
family never see fresh meat from year's end to year's
end, and that the "milk and honey" with which
the country is running, the wine itself, is either

K 2

absolutely denied, or only some of the poorest,
sourest, less wholesome quality, *mezzo-vino*, is grudg-
ingly doled out to them.   Moreover, that to such a
treatment are doomed men worn out by crushing
toil, ill-lodged, ill-clad, ill-sheltered from a climate,
the seductive smiles of which are scarcely less dangerous than its not unfrequent inclemencies.

The first care of an educating Government in Italy
should be bestowed on the people's health, and this
can only be based on their material well-being.   The
wasting malaria fever, the maddening *Pellagra*, are
ravaging the finest districts in the plain.   The *Goître,*
Cretinism, even some remnants of loathsome leprosy,
still haunt the narrow gorges of the Alps and Apen-
nines.   Statistical accounts of these dire scourges are
yearly published; learned inquiries are made as to
their nature and causes; the air, the water, all the
elements are made to bear the blame; but no one
dares to refer the evil to its true origin—to that
abject poverty, to that prostration and supineness
which has undermined the constitution of the whole
race for centuries, and exposed it, utterly defenceless,
against the most pernicious influences.   "The people
have been so accustomed," we are told.   "They are
by nature a sober, saving, self-pinching set of beings.

Even when wandering abroad for better wages, they
will over-work and starve themselves to bring home
their earnings as a provision for a rainy day." And
the Government itself, on the strength of this reasoning, and as if to encourage such delusions, insists on
keeping its soldiers on sloppy soups, on rice and paste
messes, the allowance of meat (over-boiled, never
roasted) being a few ounces less than in the French
or Austrian service. And this niggardliness they
attempt to justify on the pretext, forsooth, that a
more generous diet in barracks would not agree with
stomachs weakened by habits of abstinence at home
from childhood—an argument which it might be
worth while putting to the test of practical experiment; for, not unlikely, it would prove that it is
not the army that should be stinted, but the rural
population that should be better nourished.

Italian *polenta* (Indian meal porridge) is not worse
food than oat-meal or potato; and yet on such diet
do the Scotch and Irish peasantry manage to thrive,
and their recruits turn out as good men for a march
or a fight as their more pampered Saxon comrades.
But no unvaried diet, not even *toujours perdrix*, can
be strengthening in the long run. And the Italian
peasants, though they live not on grass, as Lady

Verney stated, have no other change than from farinaceous to vegetable food, and subsist in summer almost entirely on fruit, not unfrequently unripe and indigestible.

The question of the health and general well-being of the people, however, awaits its solution from the settlement of those economical and financial difficulties to which I have repeatedly adverted. It is a subject on which a paragraph almost invariably occurs in the King's Speech at every opening of Parliament, but on which legislation seems at a loss to come to any practical decision. Meanwhile, it seems hardly possible to believe that a rural population whom their rulers take such great pains to enable to read and write, and before whom modern progress has thrown open such easy ways of locomotion and communication with the rest of the world by land and sea, should for any length of time submit to their present condition of living. Those conditions were hardly bearable when men were tied to the soil by impassable frontier barriers, as well as by their helpless ignorance, which placed them below the rank of the black slaves in a Cuban or Brazilian plantation. But they are no longer compatible with the present order of things; and if they be insisted on, it is but natural to expect that the sufferers will either seek redress at the hand of democratic agitators, and act upon their subversive suggestions, or look for refuge in some distant land, to which railways and steamers, and the abolition of the stupid passport system now opens them a way. Symptoms of a disposition to put an end to their misery by either of those two courses, revolution or emigration, or by both, are already apparent ; for, on the one hand, reports reach us of strikes in the large cities, of subversive doctrines, and of luckily abortive but not unfrequent socialistic or communistic outbreaks here and there in Central Italy ; and, on the other, we see the South American Republics, and especially the States of the River Plate, raised to unprecedented prosperity, thanks mainly to the enormous influx of labourers of all trades from the north and south of the Italian peninsula.

Clearly the care and education of the lower classes in Italy, and especially in the country, should not altogether fall on the Government, but should also partly devolve on the upper social classes. It should rely rather on private than on public charity. There are no poor laws in that country, and the few mendicant asylums are inadequate to the need. The

mitigation of the people's sufferings is left to the
shifts of that whining street-beggary which dries up
the springs of charity in the noblest hearts, and
which degrades and depraves the paupers' character
without improving their condition. The institutions
known by the name of *Opere Pie* (Good Works),
many of them very old and well endowed, are either
under the State or Church management, and are
mostly intended for the relief of extreme want, old
age, or disabling infirmities. Their influence is not
sufficiently far-reaching and not equally diffusive,
even within the circuit of the town walls ; but beyond
it, especially after the abolition of the convents, the
land-labourer in distress can appeal to no man for
assistance except to the landowner.

And this would be a fortunate circumstance, both
for the owner and tiller of the soil, if the conditions of
agricultural industry, which is the surest and by far
the most important source of wealth for Italy, were
other than they are.

But, in the first place, the Italians are not sufficiently fond of country life ; and although necessity,
the instinct of their own interest, and an improved
sense of duty have of late tended to the prolongation
of their *villeggiatura*, still they are most of them too

poor, too desperately ground down by taxes, to afford the luxury of the *Vie de Château*, as it was in France, or of a permanent country residence as we have still in England. The abolition of the law of primogeniture had the effect of breaking up those large estates which rampant democracy denounced as the bane of the country, and the result has been a division and sub-division of property, which places the landlord almost on a level of beggary with the peasant himself. Still, no doubt, even from this, as from all other evils, it is in the power of Providence to work out some good. Necessity has sharpened the wits of the agriculturist. The wish to make the best of their altered circumstances had the effect of bringing the owner and the labourer into more constant and more intimate connexion, and making them aware of the identity of their interests. They had to lay their heads together, to inquire into the causes of distress, and to devise the remedy. A better understanding, a readier sympathy, a feeling of mutual trust and dependence rapidly sprang up between them.

That system of *mezzadria* (farming at half-profits, with rent paid not in cash, but in kind), which is not without many and serious inconveniences, has, moreover, this inestimable advantage, that the profit of the joint enterprise is greater or smaller in proportion as the partners see and know more or less of one another. The eye of the master smartens up the boor in his farm as surely as it fattens the steed in his stall. Co-operation between master and man, the intelligence of the citizen brought to bear on the practical skill of the countryman, have aroused new energies, and brightened the prospects of Italian husbandry. Within this last quarter of a century the land has been made to yield little less—perhaps more—than twice its former produce. The exportation of oil, wine, silk, cattle, fruit, etc., as we have seen,[1] has brought in money to the extent of several millions sterling; and with the improvement of agriculture most other branches of industry have shown signs of undeniable progress.

To become an instrument for the mental and moral elevation of the peasant's character, however, the townsman himself should go through a process of mental and moral, and, what is more, of physical training; and in the education of the middle and upper classes in Italy, apart from mere school learning, there is still not a little room for improvement. The Italian race, if it is to rise up to

[1] See Chapter IV., 118.

the level of its ambition, needs a great deal of
bracing up and re-invigorating. In the lower ranks
necessity for incessant work, by merely blunting the
feelings, has an almost sufficiently hardening and
chastening effect on the constitution and temperament. But among their " betters," the whole method
of bringing up seems intended to soften and unnerve,
bidding defiance to that old wholesome maxim that
" the boy is father to the man." Nowhere is
the parents' tenderness for their offspring carried
to such extremes of indulgence as in Italy, nowhere
are children more mercilessly or more hopelessly
spoilt from the cradle. An Italian mother, when a
good mother, takes pride in making herself the
indivisible companion of her progeny. From the
moment the child is taken from the breast it is
made to keep late hours, to sit up, sharing the meals
and join in the talk of grown-up people. From that
moment *il n'y a plus d'enfant.* Italian children grow
up pale and puny, but precociously wise and knowing, little prodigies, *enfants terribles;* their nerves
all developed at the expense of the muscles, ingeni-
ousness awakened to the detriment of ingenuousness.
And that same selfish, unreasoning fondness which
deals with a child as if it were a hot-house plant,

robbing it of air, light, and free movement, equally
stunts its growth at every stage of its rearing. As
there is no such place as a nursery in an Italian
household, so there is hardly a real boarding-school,
hardly a well-managed and rational collegiate institution south of the Alps. An Italian mother calls
in a private tutor, mostly a priest, for her son so
long as she can afford it, and when too poor for that,
she sends him to the gymnasium, liceum, and university of the town where she resides, and where the
organization is always on the plan and rule of a day-
school. To combine the advantages of a home with
those of a college seems to the Italians the most
plausible arrangement. But the result, to a great
extent, is to tie a youth to his mother's apron-strings,
to deprive him of every chance of learning that good
self-reliance, that regard for others, that give-and-
take sense of right and duty which make a man of
a boarding-school boy, which inure him to a hard
but wholesome discipline, and prepare him to fill the
place that awaits him in the world.

An Italian mother seems never to understand that

" Home-keeping youth have ever homely wits." [1]

---

[1] Shakespeare's 'Two Gentlemen of Verona,' Act I. sc. i. l. 2.

She is always too sure that there is contamination in all youthful intercourse. Home for the boys and a nunnery for the girls are, or have hitherto been, her ideal of a perfect family management, and the consequence is, that her daughter only too frequently comes back from her convent a frivolous bigot, and her son goes forth into the world a milksop, a muff, a coxcomb, a pigeon for the rooks to peck at, unprepared to avoid pitfalls, and resist temptations, unfit to fight the hard battles of life.

It can be no wonder if, in a race of men brought up under almost exclusive female influence, effeminacy prevails to such an extent among the males as to interfere with the fulfilment of the private and public duties incumbent on their sex. Whatever may be thought about the natural vigour of the " plant man " in Italy, there is no doubt that in the " well-to-do " classes it has been for centuries miserably vitiated. What the Italians want more than instruction is discipline. Therein lies the main difference between the Rome of the ancient Republic and the Rome of the Popes. The Italians flatter themselves that they have mustered a perfect model of a well-instructed and thoroughly disciplined army. And the army may be, for aught I know, all as it is described. But I contend that such order and drill as they have introduced, or hope to introduce into the barracks, should equally, and indeed should first, be applied to the schools. What I call education should begin in the nursery. Manly exercise should be a sacred obligation for men of all ages and all ranks.

And there really was a moment when the Italians seemed to feel where lay their sorest need, when shooting galleries, rifle companies, Alpine clubs, *Turnier-veveine*, and whatever else tends to the development of muscular strength and agility arose almost in every town of the Peninsula. But the nation, in this as in other things, seems incapable of sustained exertion. Gymnastics were soon scouted as an importation of outlandish notions. Cricket and football were English; *Turnier* was German. Why should not Italian games and sports be national?

Why indeed? Old Italy, it is true, had her own manly games. Men far advanced in life may remember the attempts made at the time of the Napoleonic wars, and continued for several years after the despotic restoration, to revive the rough sports of the Middle Ages—such sports as the "Battle of the Bridge" of Pisa, where the youth of the city, divided in two closely-packed opposite battalions, met on the height of the bridge, and strove to force back one another by sheer strength of elbows and weight of shoulders, the two contending hosts surging like ocean waves in the *mélée*, and the confused mass swaying and heaving to and fro till scores of the foremost champions on either side were fairly lifted off their feet, and went half stifled over the parapet, and down with a splash into the yellowish waves of the river beneath ;—such contests, I may add, as the schoolboy encounters of the hostile wards of the towns, *Paolotti* and *Micheletti, Barnabiti* and *Benedettini, Scozzesi* and *Inglesi,*[1] and other names, reminders of old Guelph and Ghibeline antagonism, mostly borrowed from the patron saints, the churches or convents of the various localities of most towns, the combatants all marching with their district banners at their head, led by captains made conspicuous by walking on high stilts, and carrying. on their warfare with sticks and stones, a roughish game, not without the frequent results of bloody noses and broken heads.

These sports were put an end to by the despotic governments, not only out of a reasonable regard for

---

[1] In some Italian towns divided by a river, as at Parma, the suburban quarters on the less fashionable bank of the stream are called *La Scozia,* and their denizens *Scozzesi.*

the safety of their subjects' lives and limbs, but also
from fear of the high spirits such amusements fostered
among a population about whose disaffection there
was from beginning to end no manner of doubt.
But the same objections could not be raised to other
games popular in Italy in the early part of this
century, and now utterly vanished, such as the *Trucco*,
or Billiard on the Turf, a kind of gigantic croquet,
played with enormous wooden balls, lifted with poles
having a flat ring or cup at one end, and launched
at great distance by the might of a strong arm, the
object being to drive an adversary's ball through a
revolving hoop on the ground, or to protect a ball on
which an opponent may have a similar design.   Such
as the *Pallone*, a leathern ball big and heavy enough
to crack a man's head if it alighted on it, sent to a
prodigious height by the arm, defended by an iron-
bound wooden bracelet. These, with *Tennis*, *Fives*,
and *Palla Maglio* (Pall Mall, the English name of
which still testifies its southern origin), were all games
which formed the delight of the Italian youths of
the highest ranks, especially the *Pallone*, whose
victorious champions were held in high honour, and
celebrated by Leopardi (himself debarred from such
sports by constitutional infirmity) in a strain emulous

of the odes indited by Pindar to the heroes of Olympian and Isthmian games, the patriot poet pointing to those stout gamesters as the men to whom Italy should look up for the best hopes of her future redemption.[1]

Upon political considerations, as I said, and under pretext of their dangerous character, these noble exercises were from the first discountenanced, and at last proscribed by the absolute Government of the latter days, hardly any other sports remaining than the nine-pins and bowls, the pastime of boors in their rural inns, with which the golden youths of the cities disdain to soil their dainty hands.

In their hostility to these national sports the Italian rulers of other days could always reckon on the sympathy and support of tender-hearted mothers. Pius IX. won golden opinions with the Roman matrons by forbidding the young scions of his princely families "breaking their necks" by galloping after a pack of English fox-hounds across the Campagna, only regretting that diplomatic courtesy did not allow him to extend his humane prohibition to those "heretic"

---

[1] Leopardi, Giacomo, 'Ad un Vincitore nel giuoco del Pallone, Opere,' vol. i. p. 23. Florence: 1845.

aliens who insisted on riding to the D——l, "*à l'usage de leur pays.*"

The chase, it was always contended, was the image of war, and *bella matribus detestata* has at all times been the saying in Italy; but Italian mothers should understand that war there *must* be, and that a nation not trained to it would always be, as Italy invariably was, made to bear its expenses.

Somehow, the consequences of their long period of a degrading peace had been to make the Italians of the upper classes look upon themselves as a privileged race, destined on no occasion to encounter hard knocks, debarred or exempted from military duties, and not grudging the price at which their ignoble immunity was to be purchased. Up to the end of the eighteenth century the Italians had hardly looked upon themselves as fit for the soldier's trade. The only army south of the Alps that was worth its salt was the Piedmontese, and that was not more than half Italian. That of Naples never showed its face to Championnet's *Sansculottes* in 1798, though the mere half-naked Lazzaroni rabble stood at bay at their gates, warding off the invaders for three days. From her Duchy of Milan Austria still levied good recruits among the stout Lombard peasantry; but the officers, their teachers of the fighting art, were Germans, Magyars, or Slavs, none of their own race. Genoa and Venice, though still respected at sea, enlisted Albanians or Corsicans for their land forces, and sought their safety in a policy of unarmed neutrality, which, they should have known, could only involve the loss of honour with that of their too long-protracted existence.

Deplorable days were those for poor Italy, when men were met at court, big men and officers of high birth and rank, so dead to manly shame as to talk of the *gran paura* they had had at this or that juncture, avowing their poltroonery with a naïve frankness which would hardly have been becoming silly old women, or the beardless singers of the old Papal choir.

A somewhat more manly spirit sprang up among the fallen people when Eugène Beauharnais, or Joachim Murat, dragged them after the French Imperial Eagles, giving them a flag and uniform of their own, and reviving that old name of Italy which had so long ceased to convey a meaning ; and, again, when at the close of that fitful fever, and a relapse of the Italians into their wonted sloth for half a century, another Napoleon called upon them " to be

soldiers, that they might be entitled to consider themselves men." But the Italians are now an armed
nation, and it is for the boy's home to prepare the
youth for the soldier's barracks; it is for the mother
or nurse, for the school or college, to wean, to break,
to drill and discipline the future soldier, to kill
the milksop in him, to counteract those allurements
of climate, of habit, of example, which conspire to
the precocious development of the physical propensities, at the expense and to the detriment of the
mental and moral faculties.

For all depends upon this : A sound mind can only
dwell in a sound body; the nerves must not assume too
great an ascendancy over the muscles. Italian children
are wide-awake and thinking, feeling and knowing, at
too early an age. Italian literature, as we have seen,[1]
from Boccaccio to Casti, and Italian art from Titian to
the present realistic school,[2] have always had, if not
a demoralizing, at least a debauching tendency : it
is the apotheosis of sensualism. The Tribune with
the Venuses in the picture-gallery, the ballet-girls
at the opera theatre, the novels in the library,
even the gossip in the mother's boudoir, or the
after-dinner talk in the father's smoking-room—the

[1] See *ante*, ch. iv p. 72.   [2] Chapter v. p. 108.

whole life of an Italian child at its earliest stage, seems contrived to suggest thoughts and awaken feelings, to encourage morbid passions, which no discipline in later years can have power to keep under control.

The Duchess (now Dowager Duchess) of Genoa, as a German mother (by birth a Saxon Princess), seemed well aware of the dangers and temptations besetting an Italian youth in his home education, when she sent her only son to England for a few years' experience of a Harrow school-boy's life. It would be too much, perhaps, to recommend Her Royal Highness's example to ladies of rank and fortune in Italy, to bid them tear their children from their arms, and trust them out of their sight, as English mothers must do in India, to save them from the atmospheric influences fraught with a subtle poison deadly to their tender age. It would be no easy matter to make Italian women feel how unfit soft maternal hands are to wield the rod which may prevent the spoiling of a child, and how advisable to depute the harsh but salutary use of it to a master whose affections do not run away with the sense of duty he owes to his charge. "The rod to her darling? The brute!" says the Italian mother; and that settles the question.

Boarding schools and colleges will perhaps never be popular in Italy; for the few extant institutions of that nature are mostly clerical—mere seminaries, little better than monastic prisons, of the inner conditions of which little is known, in spite of the law claiming for the authorities the right of their inspection and supervision. One can judge of them, perhaps, from the fact, that even at the royal military and naval colleges at Turin and Genoa grown-up lads of twelve to sixteen years of age are not allowed to go out alone, but must march in bands like the school-girls out of a Chiswick or Clapham academy; and never dine out, even at their parent's, or at any approved friend's houses, except under full guarantee that they shall be taken out and brought back under trusty escort, or chaperonship, no matter how short the distance, no matter how safe the road, and simply out of a vague dread of the traps and snares to which youthful inexperience and headlong passionate temperament may expose them. Such were, at least, still the rules of Italian colleges in an emancipated country only a few years ago; and in semi-jesuitical *convitti*, or boarding colleges at Turin, the same anxiety to screen ingenuous youths from all imaginable harm is still shown in the precautions

taken never to trust the students with sharp-edged
or pointed instruments, the very nail-scissors being
removed from their dressing-cases, lest, forsooth, in
some paroxysm of ungovernable fury the young
savages should inflict some grievous bodily harm
upon one another. Such absurd, and in all probability futile rules are not yet, so far as I know,
abolished; nor would it, perhaps, be advisable to do
away with them, not, at least, till the good behaviour
of the boarding students could be enforced by well-
grounded moral principles—a matter of great difficulty in a society where men will no longer acquiesce
in any sound and rational religious scheme. In these
educational matters the Italians seem unable to trace
a middle course between two opposite extremes, unable to understand that education should be neither
exclusively severe nor recklessly lax; that a college
should be neither a prison nor a road-side hotel;
that a teacher's rule in such an establishment should
be as firm and yet as light and gentle as a trainer's
hand on a colt's rein; that the rod need not strike
any more than the horse-whip, so long as the desired
effect can be obtained by merely holding it up *in
terrorem;* finally, that the necessary supervision and
guidance should never be wanting, all the time that

the student should be allowed to fancy himself free, and trusted to his own sense and discretion. In education, as in art, the hand that achieves most is that which shows itself least.[1]

In order to bring up men, the Italians will have to educate women. The practice of immuring tender girls into a nunnery till the time comes to give them up to a husband they have never seen or heard of is being rapidly discontinued; and very creditable free lay institutions for the instruction of girls of every rank and condition of life are rising in almost every important town in the Peninsula; in addition, not in opposition, to the establishments under the management of the Ursuline and other pious nuns not suppressed. Still, the notion that the mother's home is the best school for a girl to be reared in is almost universally prevalent; and it would be a golden rule if the mother were in all cases wise and able, to adopt with her daughter any good method of bringing up in which she had herself been trained. But a girl in Italy is too generally looked upon as the most brittle piece of china, which the least touch can crack, as the purest crystal mirror that the faintest breath can tarnish. Home is no better than a convent, if a girl

---

[1] 'L'arte che tutto fa nulla si scopre,' Tasso, Canto xvi. st. ix.

is to be guarded in it as in a harem. The absurdity
of an old maid of forty or fifty dreading to lose caste
if she is seen venturing out alone in the streets, and
yet thinking she is all right if she appears under
the chaperonship of a matron (be she even a young
wife of eighteen or twenty), ought to be sufficiently
glaring ; and, indeed, sounder ideas begin to prevail.
But the old prejudice had its origin in that looseness
of manners, in that excess of gallant staring admiration, void of chivalrous respect, with which an
unprotected female is too often treated in southern
countries, and of which free and proud beauties from
colder climates have only too good reason to complain.
It is one of those vicious relics of the past, of which
Italy can never be too heartily ashamed, if there be
any reality in her aspirations to a better future.

In the case of a well-educated nation, as of a well-
managed household, the intercourse between the sexes
should be regulated upon the general principles of
action and reaction. Women are always what men
make them, or what men wish them to be, and *vice-
versâ*. The *lion* is no lion if he be not at *Una's* feet ;
Una is not Una if she can have no faith in the lion's
respect and devotion. That Italy may be great it is
necessary that she should establish the true woman-

worship ; that woman should know how to assert and
deserve her proper ascendancy. It is necessary that
the same principles of physical and moral education,
though in different degrees, should be applied to both
sexes. In a girl as in a boy, a healthy mind in a
healthy body should be equally cultivated. Neither
of them should be deprived of those blessings of free
air and cold water, of those wholesome and strengthening habits of riding and swimming, of skating and
boating and other exercises which they can enjoy,
jointly or separately ; neither of them should be
debarred from a careful initiation in the knowledge of
good and evil. Both should be brought up as intelligent, responsible beings ; within reasonable limits, as
self-relying, free agents. Both should be taught to
dread to do evil, and to have no other fear.

CHAPTER VII.

SOCIETY.

THE further I advance towards the accomplishment of my task, the larger becomes the number and the graver the nature of the questions to which I must find an answer.

What are the Italians of the present day like? In what do they differ from what they were before their new existence began? What will they become upon an indefinite continuation of their present condition? What will they be like half a century hence, when the generation which witnessed this comparatively peaceful revolution shall have altogether been struck out of the roll of the living?

In the first place, I think that it would be hardly fair to judge of the Italians as they are from what they are supposed to have been ; foreign ethnologists, for the most part, seem to think they can save the trouble of becoming acquainted with the character of the living by referring to the memorials of the dead. They rely on history, their history, compiled out of such records as former generations left of themselves— pictures, in the case of Italy, made out of the portraits friends and enemies, Guelphs and Ghibelines, drew of each other, about as true to nature as would be a likeness of a Disraeli done by a Whig, or of a Gladstone done by a Tory print, or the caricature of either of them appearing in a cartoon of ' Punch' before photography came to his aid.

I suppose we know about Cæsar Borgia as much as we do about King Richard III. Why should we then be sure that the former had his brother drowned in the Tiber, while we are so sceptic about the latter smothering his nephews in the Tower? That the Italians of the Middle Ages were as great monsters of depravity as they were prodigies of intelligence may be true. Only, as to their intelligence, that may be gauged from their works ; but as to their character, that is an affair of history, which is the same thing as to say, a matter of doubt. And it may well be that the impression we have of mediæval times is owing not to the fact that the Italians were then so much better or so much worse than other people, but that they thought and talked and wrote so much more, and that there was in what they said and left written more of that passion, more of that blind love or hatred, more of that base flattery and of that black calumny than occurs in the records of less advanced and less intellectually active communities. At every step we make in our improvement of historical criticism, we feel inclined to think more charitably even of that wretched Spanish Papal family, the Borjas, or Borgias. Cæsar may have been as black as he is painted ; but as to Lucretia, after all that has been said, from Roscoe to Gregorovius, we must avow that her guilt or innocence is as problematic as that of Mary Stuart. How can either fair or foul ever be made out of witnesses which it is now no longer in our power to cross-question ?

But whatever we may believe or disbelieve of the Italians of the Renaissance, it is idle to imagine that there is much, or indeed anything in common between them and the Italians of the present day. There is not only difference, but perfect contrast

between the two races. With the Mediæval Italians
the fault lay in an excess of energy ; the life that was
in them wore itself out in fratricidal and suicidal
strife. They had to struggle against foreign domination, they conspired against each other's independence ; days of union had strengthened them, ages
of discord exhausted, annihilated them. The overweening sense of individual power blinded them to
the necessity of joint action and mutual reliance.

The present Italians, on the other hand, have a
humble but salutary consciousness of their own weakness. They are aware that they longed, they suffered,
but did not fight (at least only an inconsiderable
number of them fought) for their freedom. The rise
of the Italian kingdom was the work of a *Plebiscite*,
of the clamour of a Neapolitan mob ; it was owing
to the oversight of an effete diplomacy, to a hitch
in the gear of the European balance of power.
Solferino, in the opinion of some cool-headed politicians, was as " untoward an event," *i. e.* as egregious
a blunder as Navarino. Only the Italians had better
luck, or perhaps more readiness to make the best
of their opportunity than their Greek brethren. A
great miracle was performed in behalf of Italy ; her
worst enemies turned out her best friends. The

Italians are the first and only people whose victory was completed by a defeat.

And the Italians know all this ; in their weakness, they feel, lies their necessity for union. When Victor Emmanuel proclaimed that Italy should aspire to be "not only respected, but also *feared*," he only expressed a wish, a distant hope. For the present the Italian kingdom is armed by land and sea : time alone will show what use it may make of its weapons.

The energies of a nation need not always be roused by wars or revolutions; indeed, the nature of such awakening is often too violent, its results too uncertain, and even on the most favourable issue, too disastrous and ruinous for any nation to wish to hasten its outbreak. Italy's mission, it was understood from the beginning, was to be pacific ; by all means let her make herself strong, but let trust and love rather than fear be the feelings Italy inspires. Her French neighbours tried all that vapouring and *Chauvinism* could do ; and what good did the experiment ever do them ?

Before the Italians resort to trials of strength for the rehabilitation of their national character, let them see what can be achieved to the same effect by their proficiency in the arts of peace ; let them show how much can be accomplished by the means of a wise Government and a still wiser education. My opinion of what the Italians have hitherto done in that respect may be read in the foregoing chapters. My further object in this is to inquire to what extent both Government and education have as yet in Italy influenced social organization.

Self-government does not come to a nation by mere intuition; it is the result of long, patient, and not unfrequently painful experience. But in order that success may attend it, self-government must be the nation's own work; and unfortunately the Italians, pressed for time, were in too great a hurry to borrow their notions of good government from abroad, chiefly from France. Suffering for so many years from German or Austrian rule, they had accustomed themselves to look to France for deliverance. With Vienna they associated all their ideas of obscurantism; all light was expected from Paris. Their first cry was for "Liberty as in France," and that was *equality, democracy, down with the aristocracy;* in other words, a war of classes.

In every state the Government should be in the hands of the *Aristoi,* or *best* men; but these, Mazzini taught, were no longer to be looked for among the members of the present Italian nobility. They were too numerous, their titles were too lavishly extended to all the scions of the same families, and many of them were too idle, too effeminate, too bigoted to supply the elements of a governing class.

There is a great deal of truth in all that. But even admitting that such is the rule, there is no reason why the exception should be overlooked, no reason why it should, à priori, be taken for granted that a man must needs be an idiot or a bigot, from the mere fact that he is a noble, and *that* in the land of Cavour and D'Azeglio, of Ricasoli and Capponi.

The oldest nobility, whatever may be said to their disparagement, is yet what remains most genuine Italian in Italy. Their ranks have been thinned, their lustre has been outshone by new men, their order has been invaded by the bribery the Government accepts for the honours of which the King is supposed to be the fountain; they have been impoverished, ground to dust by the law of succession, imposing incessant division and subdivision of property; but they still bear in their stature or their features, in their manners, in their principles, the traces of what is most remarkable, most respectable in the national character.

They are not easily come at by foreign visitors, not often to be met in the Quirinal ante-chambers, nor any longer (except the older members, or the ladies of their families) in those of the Vatican. They are apt to hide their diminished heads in tumble-down palaces, in decayed towns of obscure provinces, nursing the mere wrecks of their shattered estates, patching them up by intermarriages, by strict and even sordid economy, by every contrivance of natural and even unnatural self-denial.

Nothing more depressing, nothing more distressing than a visit to the inmates of one of these Italian St. Germain Faubourgs. You must look for them in some old mansion, of which the best available suites on the ground floor, or the *Piano Nobile*, are most likely taken up for Diligence or Railway *Bureaux*, or for the Gresham or Phœnix Life and Fire Insurance offices. You have to grope under lofty portals, along dimly-lighted vestibules and corridors; not unlikely across damp and mouldy courts, three in succession, till you come to some pavilion at the back, where you are ushered in by an old footman in faded livery, and find the family huddled together in musty chambers, possibly the former abode of the domestic establishment where they have their only sitting-room, but where the faded tapestry, the dingy portraits, the four-wick silver oil-lamp, with some oak chest, or ivory in-laid cabinet, or the like heirlooms still bear evidence of departed greatness and lingering taste.

You find the old patrician in winter seated near the dark, bare chimney, wrapped in his long-skirted overcoat, or padded brocade dressing-gown and furred slippers, wearing, if not his hat, his black velvet embroidered skull-cap; entertaining, may be, at his *Tresette*, or whist-table, the notary, the doctor, or some other professional (admitted officially, as it were, as former dependants of the household, and still its grateful and obsequious clients), his woman-kind trying not to shiver, with the hands on their *scaldinos*, and the *chaufrettes* at their feet, as they ply their crochet 'needles or embroidery frames; while the family chaplain, a never-failing attendant, a mass-priest, and confessor *dalla manica larga* (broad-sleeved, *i.e.* not sticking at trifles in dealing out absolution), bustles about from group to group, the most jocular man of the party, looking over the players' hands, or inspecting the ladies' work, with the occasional comment of a licensed jester.

This is a chilly and dingy piece of still life—a sad exhibition of the havoc of old Italy with which

you will not easily become acquainted unless you
wander a great deal out of the usual tourist track.
But this is only the dark side of the picture.   There
is a living as well as a dead nobility in Italy.   Not
unlikely the eldest, or may be the only son of that
desolate household, which we have seen hiding
from the light like an owl's nest in their provincial
retirement, is at the very moment seeking distinction
in the army or navy, or in the Diplomatic or Consular
service.   Perhaps he is on the eve of re-gilding his
father's coronet by a *mésalliance,* thanks to which
we shall soon see him doing grand in the palace
over his father-in-law's banking house at Milan, or
at that millionnaire's sumptuous villa near Como.   A
mere title is in itself worse than worthless in Italy,
but it is still something to have one's lineage in ' Litta's
Peerage,' not of noble, but "celebrated" families.
It may even, in some cases, be a distinction to have,
like the Peruzzi, no handle to one's name.   But the
Italians are proud of their history, and they gauge
the honours of their nobles from the records of their
historical ancestry.   Such honours may be perpetuated in the male or female lines.   It may matter
little whether a Torlonia calls himself a Colonna in
his own or in his wife's right; but there is no doubt

that the banker's wealth is doubled in social value by its connection with a real Prince's descent. The vicissitudes of fortune and the upward instincts of race will always tend, even in the most hopelessly democratized community, to keep up that ascending and descending scale which in England is the result of the wise organization of her open aristocracy.

At Milan, at Florence, and in other large cities, centres of broad territories, where the estates are indivisible by the very nature of their only practicable cultivation, there will always be great landowners, no matter how often the properties may have to change hands, no matter how necessary the proprietors may find it to eke out their agricultural income by the auxiliary product of trading or financial speculation.

Now it has been justly stated by Foscolo,[1] at the very moment the last spark of old Italian life was expiring at Venice, that "there may be a country without inhabitants, but no nation can ever exist without land. Consequently the few great lords of the soil in Italy must for ever be the visible or invisible rulers and heads of the people." Italy is

---

[1] Foscolo, Ugo, 'Ultime lettere di Iacopo Ortis,' Lett. of March, 1798, Florence, 1850, page 41.

and can only be an agricultural country, and her
husbandry in the most fertile districts can only
thrive on a system of cultivation on a large scale.
There must, therefore, be great landowners, and these,
whether they belong to the nobility of ancient date,
or whether they be new men stepping into their
places by family connections (as the Smithson Smith
were grafted on the Percies), or finally mere upstarts
with not a speck of the dust of time on their cheaply
bought coronets, will be sure to constitute the actual
aristocracy of the country; the men of ancient
descent leavening the whole mass, and at the third
or fourth generation assimilating all the less pure
heterogeneous elements.

This aristocracy may, for a time, either by the
envious opposition of a rampant democracy, or by
their own indolence and love of ease, be debarred
from the exercise of that political influence which
naturally belongs to them. But nothing can deprive
them of that social ascendancy, of that leadership
of fashion and opinion, which must in the long run
enable them to recover the upper hand in the management of public affairs, in spite even of the violent
revolution or of the fraudulent legislation which
conspires to rob them of it.

It is important to observe, that even of the older Italian families of illustrious descent, but few belong to the so-called *nobiltà castellana*, feudal or country nobility. Life in Italy was for centuries mere city life. The nobles were simply patricians, conspicuous citizens, but citizens; and it was a common saying among them that "Trade soils no man's hands."[1] The Benso (Cavour) of Chieri, the Alfieri of Asti, the Bardi and Peruzzi of Florence, however blue might be the blood in their veins, whatever castles and estates they might possess in the country, to whatever rank they might rise at Court or in the State, were mainly indebted for their greatness to their business as money-lenders, bankers, financiers. Even at the present time, at the back of the Ridolfi, Ricasoli, and other Florentine palaces there are little wicket-gates or shop-doors, where the retail-trade in oil and wine from the great man's farms and vineyards is, as it always was, carried on. The sheer poverty with which the law of divided inheritance threatens the Italian noblest families cannot fail to put them on their mettle, supplying that stimulus to exertion which they hitherto so sorely wanted. Many of them, if not all of them (for the Cavour,

---

[1] " Il commercio non isporca le mani a nessuno."

D'Azeglio, Alfieri, etc., as if disdaining to resign themselves to their fallen state or diminished lustre, eschew marriage, and seem bent on self-extinction), many of them, I say, will know how to make the best of the altered circumstances of the new social order, and will be sure to emerge from the obscurity into which the insane theories of French equality threaten to plunge not only Italy and the other Latin communities, but even Gladstone's England.

Next in importance to the great owners of the soil must be in Italy its cultivators, the labourers, who, as we have seen,[1] make up more than half of the population.

The Italian peasantry, now the slave of want and ignorance, are the direct descendants of the slaves or captives imported into the country by the victories of Imperial Rome, taking the place of the free men used up to supply her legions in her incessant wars —an alien race, originally from remote provinces, mixed up with the legionaries themselves, among whom the vacant land was distributed, and most of whom were in later times men of northern or eastern, of any but the "gentle Latin blood;" the whole mass in the end trodden down and rough-

[1] See Vol. I. chap. iv. p. 105.

ridden by the Goths, Vandals, and Langobards of the barbaric inroads, who seized the land, squatted upon it, shared it with the vanquished hinds whom they found in possession, and with whom they claimed kindred, amalgamating with them, and acknowledging as their common masters and feudal lords the warrior chiefs who had led the nomadic hosts to the conquest.

From that time, *i. e.* from the formation of the modern nation, there was antagonism in Italy between the town and country population. For on the breaking up of the feudal system, and at the rise of the free cities, the nobles, from choice or necessity, abandoning their castles, settled in the towns, and fraternized with the citizens, some of their feudal possessions becoming the property either of the Church or of the community in which they, the nobles themselves, had chosen their abode.

The poor peasant, neutral and passive in all that violent change, was left out in the cold, claiming no other right on the land than that of tilling it, and sharing its produce with any who might call himself master, however little the new-comer might be known to him. Debarred from public life by his isolated position, the first exposed to the outrages of the frequent foreign invasions, but less immediately harassed by the vexations of home mismanagement, the Italian rustic had learnt from the experience of ages to remain unmoved and unconcerned in all the country's vicissitudes, accepting accomplished facts, submitting to established authority, consoling himself with the philosophy of Æsop's beast of burden, "that he had only one back, and no new master could make him bear two loads," and seeing little to choose between French and German, Spanish or Austrian rule, so long as he had enough to eat; the old refrain being,

"Vegna la Franza, vegna la Spagna,
    Mi no m'importa, basta ch'a magna." [1]

It is upon this inert and unwieldy rural multitude that the Italian electoral law, after endless modifications, all in ultra-Radical sense, has lately extended the franchise almost on the basis of absolute manhood suffrage.   It is needless to say that, *motu proprio*, the Italian boor would little care to know how to choose his Parliamentary representative.   Left to himself, he would only be anxious to escape the trouble of walking to the poll.   There seems as

[1] "Let France, let Spain, let come who will,
    So I am left to eat my fill."

yet to be too much honesty, too little ambition, or too little money in Italy for any man to resort to bribery on the scale that the crowd of voters would now-a-days require. Nor is it easy for the demagogue to find arguments to pierce the density of the poor countryman's muddled brain, and the only chance of influencing his vote rests with the priest, the only semi-civilized being who lives among his flock from year's end to year's end, who as a rule springs from their ranks, and identifies himself with them ; but who is advised to be neutral in all controversies unless an opportunity offers to put in a word for the Pope, denouncing the Godless Government, and creating alarm about the eventual suppression of the Mass, which is the peasant's greatest need after his daily bread.

Clearly the political power in the present organization of Italy resides in neither of the two opposite poles of society. Not in the decayed, envied, and spitefully cried-down nobility, nor in the helpless and stolidly unimpressionable rural population ; but between them, between the land-owners and the land-labourers, lies the whole middle class of the towns, those whom it is usual to designate as "The People."

"Lawyers and doctors," said Foscolo,[1] "professors of the universities, with the whole swarm of high or low public functionaries, are engaged in what they call gentlemanly pursuits; but they have not, for all that, the position and influence of real gentlemen. Whoever earns by his own personal industry, be it bread, be it gold, and owns no land, is only one of the people" (*non è se non parte di plebe*), "a better-off class of people may be, but not more free" (*plebe meno misera, non già meno serva*).

With the ideas of nearly ninety years since, Foscolo had evidently no faith in the *bourgeoisie* as a governing class; and the experience made of that set of people in France during the eighteen years of the so-called "July Monarchy" would certainly, had he lived to see it, not have increased his respect for *bourgeois* rule. That rule could not, at all events, be encouraging to those among France's neighbours who, like the Italians, have too long been and are striving to organize themselves on the French plan. From the middle class in France the Government fell into the hands of the lower orders; from the "citizen-King" to the "République Ouvrière" (1848 —1852); and from this, again, after the "Empire

---

[1] Foscolo, 'Ortis,' *loc cit.*

des Filous" (1852—1870) to the "Commune," or, in short, from the *bourgeoisie* to the *canaille*.

Whether owing to her good fortune, or to her sounder political instincts, Italy has hitherto stopped short on the brink of this perilous slope. But it would be rash to "cry wool ere we are well out of the wood." Foscolo had no reliance on a government of advocates and professors, the men now at the head of Italian democracy, and, in my opinion, for very good reasons; and, for the best, that even if they had the abilities, these worthies would not have the training and temper, would not have the leisure to take upon themselves the management of public affairs, as would be the case with men to the manner born.

Foscolo had wisely drawn the line, and traced the definition of aristocratic government as it should be. The "best men," *cæteris paribus*, will prove to be those whose bread has been earned either by their own or by their fathers' exertions—men placed above want, and, as a rule, above temptation, and who, free from care about their own means of subsistence, can turn all their energies to the promotion of the common weal. Consciousness of authority, habits of command best comes to him who feels surest of his social position; not to the merchant, whose thoughts are with his argosies "tossing on the ocean," not to the lawyer or doctor, or other professional, whose earnings depend on his mental and bodily health, and on the terms he is on with his clients, and who can hardly emancipate himself from his private duties without incurring losses for which he will claim the right of indemnifying himself at the public expense. Patriotism may be very strong in the poor man's heart, but charity begins at home. A poor man may step forward in great emergencies, he may volunteer to act as a ruler, as he would fight as a soldier in some supreme crisis; but in the long run, and in normal times, men who have to look to "the main chance" had better leave government, as they would leave military service after the war, to those whose circumstances enable them to take up such pursuits as their own special occupation.

The worst of it is, that with the middle class at the head of the Government, State affairs are liable to fall from the management of those who have too little leisure to attend to them to those who have rather too much time to bestow upon them—to the doctors lacking patients, and the lawyers waiting for briefs. In the absence of those *best men* who ought to be *statesmen by position*, we have but too often those (the very *worst*) who make themselves *politicians by trade.*

The middle class in Italy constitutes a much more extensive multitude than it does in other countries, as, for instance, in England; for it recruits its ranks from the two opposite poles of society, from the highest and lowest orders. On the one hand, the great land-owners, be they old nobles, or merely upstarts, having their homes in the towns, evince a tendency to lose caste by familiar intercourse, and even by intermarriage with those of lower degree; and, on the other hand, the peasantry, driven by want, or lured by vague hopes of "bettering themselves," flock to the cities, where they can only swell the ranks and aggravate the miseries of the town proletariat. Italian life is thus, in reality, nearly all city life, in a great measure all middle class life. The general tendency of society, and of the Government at the head of it, is *à s'encanailler*, i. e. to rub off all distinctions, to establish that democratic equality which sinks from a low to a lower level, and only stops at the lowest.

The social world, like the material, obeys the impulse of centrifugal and centripetal forces, in a

perpetual succession of action and reaction. When
it has long enough followed the impulse in one
direction it is apt to set off at a tangent on the
opposite. Socially as well as politically, Italy is only
too ready to follow democratic France; but even in
the blindness of her imitative instincts, she draws
the line somewhere, and acts upon her own cooler
and sounder judgment, not only avoiding hitherto
all France's fatal blunders, but managing to profit
by the lessons which are derived from them.

For luckily, after all, though the nature of the
two countries is similar, it is not exactly identical.
Like France, Italy is an agricultural country; but she
is not, like France, agricultural and something else.
The Italians of the present day, as we have seen,
show little aptitude for either trade or industry on
a large scale. The division of the country into small
states had for a long time contracted their views,
crippled their energies, and narrowed their field of
enterprise. For the present no very great fortunes
are made by extensive manufacturing or commercial
speculation. The instincts of the mere shopkeeper
or pedlar characterized the Italian trader both at
home and abroad, even, as we have seen,[1] in those

[1] See Vol. I. ch. vi. pp. 149, 150.

South-American Republics, where he is the one-eyed man in the land of the blind. The few staple articles of manufacture that Italy contributes to the marts of the world, such as silk, Tuscan straw hats (an industry now on its last legs), stone and coral work, etc., are either raw material, or are exported in the most rudimentary state of preparation, to receive form and finish abroad. The universal complaint in Italy is want of capital. As in Spain, Greece, or Turkey, most of the Italian banking and wholesale commercial business, of railway, canal, and mining enterprise, is either in the hands of aliens, or relies on strong alien connection and support.

Ultimately, however, it is the soil that must bear the costs. Italian wealth is, and may perhaps for ever be, almost exclusively agricultural, and the main question is, in whose possession the land may and must remain. By far the most considerable and productive part of the Italian plain is arable and grazing land, and can best thrive by the cultivation of grain, milk and dairy produce on a large scale. The great land-owners will, therefore, always have the lion's share of Italian wealth, and of such power, actual or virtual, as wealth may wield in the State; but in hilly districts, and in the immediate neighbourhood of the large towns, the soil is often turned to the purposes of flower and vegetable gardens, nursery grounds, vineyards and orchards, olive and orange-groves; and there the land admits of almost endless division and subdivision.

The experiment of peasant proprietorship has not as yet been tried in Italy, and will probably never be attempted ; for by the *mezzadria*, or half-profits of culture indigenous and characteristic of that country, the land-labourer feels that he is co-proprietor with his employer, and that where the system works well no change could better his position. The *mezzadria* system does not always work as well as it might and should do, but it is admirably contrived for the co-operation of capital and labour to a common purpose, and works best where the husbandry is conducted on an extensive plan, and where the profit depends on the amount of the expenditure. Abandoned to his own resources, the Italian peasant-proprietor could only live from hand to mouth, and would soon fall into the clutches of the usurer, never to extricate himself from them. A wise Italian land-owner finds it for his own interest to treat his *mezzadro* at least as humanely as this latter, also for his own advantage, treats his cattle. To make the

system work well it is only necessary that the landlord's means should be adequate to the requirements
of the husbandry, that the intercourse between master
and man should be direct and constant, and that the
owner should take upon himself the management,
and reside for at least a part of the year on his
estate as his own agent. To this arrangement many
of the upper classes are and will be brought by their
gradual yet rapid impoverishment.

But besides the great land-owners, there is in Italy
a very extensive class of small landed proprietors (the
owners of the soil constitute a population altogether
reckoned at 1,875,238 souls), and it is among the
minor landlords that the zone of land round the
towns is mainly parcelled. There are in most Italian
towns, especially in the smaller ones, numbers of
petty tradesmen and well-to-do mechanics or artisans,
professional men, government officials of various
rank, and the like—men who will often stint and
deny themselves to any extent for the satisfaction of
having their own little campagna, their acre or two,
as they say, *al sole*, in the sun. They have hardly
ever a home, and seldom more than a *pied à terre*
(*spogliatoio*, or disrobing room they call it), outside
the town-walls; for even the most elegant citizen-

boxes or sumptuous suburban villas in Italy are neither fitted nor intended for permanent habitation, at least during the winter, and are destitute of what would be considered comfort in England at all seasons. But the townsman must have his freehold, where he may send his wife and children "to enjoy a breath of free air, and to eat their figs and grapes off the tree with the dew on the .fruit, on a fine autumn morning," and where he may gather friends and relatives to a Sunday picnic "under the shade of his own vine arbour." The owner himself is not often an amateur gardener, or experimental agriculturist; the cultivation of his plot of ground, if it be of any worth, is entrusted to a labourer, who may reside on or near the spot, or even have his lodgings in the back slums of the town, and go out daily at any hour of the day, in some cases having the care, not only of one, but of several of these small suburban holdings, on *mezzadro* terms, paying generally in kind to each of his employers the due share of the produce.

On these terms, the more the extent of the great old estates diminishes, the more the relations between town and country becomes frequent and intimate. Land on a small scale is coveted by the middle and lower classes, not only for pleasure and as a luxury, but also as a safe and not unprofitable investment, as it seldom yields less than 4 per cent., and in the vicinity of towns, if used for flower and kitchen garden, or nursery, and well watered, 6 per cent. and upwards.

And for this latter purpose, as a speculation, there have of late been causes tending to carry out the system much further by this same class of people, and to apply it to the same kind of property on far more considerable proportions. For of the Church and State lands, which were thrown into the markets at low prices, and on a variety of advantageous terms, on the annexation of all Italy to Piedmont in 1860, but little could be purchased *en bloc* by private persons, but had to be put up by auction in small lots, which were bought on speculation, not by the peasants themselves (who are mostly penniless), but more generally by moneyed citizens, either singly, or in joint-stock companies, and by these either given out as farms to the peasants on the usual half-profit arrangement, or placed under the management of some land-agent, steward, or "secretary" (*Mercante di Campagna* is the name in Rome), who returns in money to each of the owners a yearly percentage for his respective share of the capital.

The division of property, imposed in Italy by the law of inheritance, had no doubt the fatal effect of breaking up many large and handsome patrimonies; but by way of some compensation, the land-hunger awakened among new men, bringing into the management of their properties ampler and readier means, greater thrift, and superior intelligence, will tend to a contrary and more satisfactory result; to the piecing and patching together of the fragments of fallen fortunes, in the preservation and improvement of which sterner energies will be enlisted. And the example of these upstarts will, it may be hoped, not be wholly lost among the disinherited scions of the former proprietors. Reconstruction will thus, in some measure, keep pace with disintegration and dissolution. And in the struggle and emulation between the old and new landowners, the land itself and the land-labourer will be the gainers. For the eternal principle, that property has its duties as well as its rights, will be more fully understood and acted upon, and among the most stringent obligations will be that of a more just and humane treatment of the poor peasantry, of their rise in the scale of human beings, of a more frequent intercourse between them and their employers. There will ensue a keener sense of common interests, livelier sympathies, greater mutual trust and dependence ; above all things, a gradual disappearance of middle men, and the necessity for the landlord of a prolonged residence on his estate, and of a more immediate and assiduous attention to his business.

For, be it observed, it is not altogether because the Italians are insensible to the blessings of fresh air, fine scenery, field sports, thorough peace and freedom, and all the infinite charms of country life, that they cling so obstinately to their towns in those hot months, when the stifling atmosphere becomes almost pestilential, leaving them only for a short spell of *villeggiatura* late in autumn, when people huddle together at their bathing-places among parched hills, or on the dusty and sun-burnt shore of a tepid sea. No ; the absenteeism of the owners, which is as injurious to landed property in Italy as it is in Ireland, arises from other causes besides the want in the country of the café, the theatre, and other resorts, which long habit has made a necessity for an Italian. It arises from a vague but general feeling of insecurity ; from the dread of that brigandage which in some of the provinces has not yet been wholly extirpated, and still more from the deficiency in the Italian rural districts of those domestic comforts and luxuries which follow an Englishman even into the remotest and most lonely country abode ; for the lack of that enterprise, diligence, and punctuality of butchers, grocers, and all provision dealers, to say nothing of those co-operative stores, of those circulating libraries, and other similar contrivances which, aided by the improvement and extension of all means of communication, enable John Bull to make himself at home in the quietest and apparently most helpless solitude.

These advantages of a more forward civilization are gradually winning their way into Italy, and will soon make the Italians take to and delight in their country residences. Italy is now going through a silent and peaceful social revolution, which will make the people aware of the treasure they have buried in the soil of the country, and convince them that they have only to dig deeper and deeper to get at the amplest and safest sources of national wealth. The improvement of husbandry in all the northern and central provinces of the Peninsula is, as I stated, everywhere apparent ; and there is a visible progress in the colonization and cultivation, the actual peaceful and beneficent conquest of the south by emigrants from the north. The Italians, like other people, will learn to love, honour, and encourage agriculture in proportion as it is made worth their while to take to it. They will harbour no fear of the competition of cheap Russian or American corn. Wheat will never fall so low in price as to be given to fatten pigs with it, as it is done in England ; for although Cavour had made a Free Trade policy a fashion and a madness in Italy in Cobden's time, the Italians have too much common sense to hesitate about any measure required for the protection of their landed interests, from a silly fear of the charge of inconsistency in their principles of political economy. Nothing is less likely to repair an error than blind perseverance in it. The Italians well know that the produce of the land is the first, the surest, and most inalienable source of any nation's wealth, and that to it all other interests should be made subservient.

Hitherto hardly more than half has been done in Italy towards the promotion of national agricultural resources. War has yet to be waged against that direst of all scourges, the malaria. Where the Italians do not subdue their own land, the land kills them ; where malaria is not driven back, it is sure to gain ground.

With good management and perseverance Italy
may be made to double her agricultural produce, both
as to quantity and quality.   And when this exceeds,
as it must to a considerable extent, the exigencies of
home consumption, we have seen that Italy can be
at no loss for good foreign markets.   The interchange
of commodities between the north and south, the
east and west of Europe is one of the least foreseen,
but of the most important and satisfactory results
of the great political changes of which these last
five-and-twenty years have been witnesses, and more
especially of the rise of a united Italy and a united
Germany and the limitation of the overbearing arro-
gance of France and Russia ; a rearrangement of the
balance of power against which it is devoutly to be
hoped that neither the restlessness of the former nor
the faithlessness of the latter of these two Powers,
will ever have a chance of prevailing.

Meanwhile, that the rising and the future generations of Italy will be socially better off than they
have ever been, need not be doubted.   It only
remains to be seen to what extent moral improvement will keep pace with the development of material
well-being.

CHAPTER VIII.

CHARACTER.

THE moral character of a nation is, before all things,
matter of race; but it is in some measure affected by
geographical position, by soil and climate, and other
material circumstances over which men can exercise
no unlimited control, and it is further modified by
civil, social, and religious institutions for which they
are only responsible to the extent that they are able
to maintain the free and independent guidance of
their own destinies.

The Italians are perhaps the most mixed and varied

population in Europe; the outcome of incessant invasions by land and sea, both before and after they were united under Roman sway, and hardly ever belonging to themselves till Solferino and Sedan providentially rid them of their last Austrian and French intruders. But there is, nevertheless, a national character in Italy, and it bears to a great extent its own peculiar original mark, distinguishable in the north by a prevalence of Celtic and Germanic blood, and in the south by the admixture of Greek and Moorish, and other Asiatic and African elements.

And the lines of demarcation are still the same as they were in ancient Roman times, traceable on the eastern side, at the Rubicon (now Fiumicino), near Rimini, where the clipped and twisted but strong and expressive dialect, and the Gallic nasal twang of the Lombard and Emilian come into contact, but never blend with the soft but monotonous drawl of the Marches; and on the western side, at the Magra near Sarzana, where the uncouth but energetic Ligurian borders on the more elegant, but hardly more euphonious Etruscan; and further south, on the Ombrone, below Siena, where the guttural Tuscan idioms melt in the pure and musical accent of the Eternal City.

South of Rome, again, the Neapolitan pronunciation has not a few peculiarities, revealing the hereditary formation of the original Hellenic (Doric) organ, in the softened consonants of such words as Tan*d*o for Tan*t*o, *Chiaia* for *Piag*gia, *chiag*nere for *piang*ere, inter*pet*rare for inter*pret*are, etc.; while at Palermo in Sicily, Cagliari in Sardinia, and Aiaccio in Corsica, the vowels uttered through the closely pursed-up lips, the *u* for *o* (T*u*sco for T*o*sco, Ragi*u*ni for Ragioni, C*u*rso for Corso, lett*u* for letto, etc.), tell of the long residence first of the Saracens, then of the Aragonese, in the islands.

As in the language, so in the features, in the eyes and hair, in the complexion and the whole cast of countenance, the change at every step, with almost every degree of latitude, is equally observable, the difference of type striking the eye as forcibly as the variety of accent affects the ear.

The Italians are certainly not the handsomest people in the world; beauty is by no means so common among them as it is in the north, and especially in England (the land of roast meat, pudding, and wholesome ale). But from the midst of an ill-fed, ill-washed, and vitiated multitude, there flash forth here and there in that southern land such rare prodigies both of male and female perfection of face and figure, such paragons of colour, such miracles of eyes, as hardly any other nation can rival or even approach. It is the loveliness which supplied the great masters of the various schools of Italian art with their matchless models; the schools of Rome, Florence, Milan, Parma, Bologna, etc., each with its peculiar type of a Madonna or a Magdalen, of a Cupid or an angel, or a heaven-born infant,—all ideals of which the various localities still exhibit the perhaps more rare but not less undeniable original pattern.

And as in the outward look, so in the inner constitution of the mind and heart of the Italian people, the same variety and contrast between the opposite extremes of good and evil, of virtue and vice, will occur, more observable perhaps than in less mixed races. One will find rare specimens of moral excellence by the side of hideous depravity of disposition. This, we may be told, must be the case wherever men are; but it is especially so in southern climates, where greater intensity of feeling is found in combination with greater subtlety of intelligence, and where the control over the passions is with more difficulty established or maintained. The sun must bear his part both of the merit and blame.

With respect to natural gifts, the Italians will impress a stranger with the more favourable opinion the farther he proceeds from north to south ; but the reverse will be his experience of all that relates to culture, order, and the commonest decencies of life. Civilization will strike him as most backward, where its influence, if properly applied, ought to have given the most signal results. In a progress from Milan to Naples a traveller's sensations will be the same as he might experience in a journey from the best English counties to the wildest Irish districts.

English visitors in Italy do not, for the most part, take these differences into account. For them, whatever they see in Italy is simply Italian. What hitherto brought them across the Alps, besides their love of the country and climate, was a somewhat vague pity for the sufferings of "a noble though fallen people." But now that people is up again erect and free, and its nobleness, in the opinion of these same benevolent strangers, is, one would say, less apparent. The Italians have risen to the rank of a self-governing nation,—one of those nations sympathy with which must be based on respect. Travellers do not find fault with the Italians, but they have ceased to trouble themselves much or little about them. The interest felt for them has in a very great measure died off.

The worst of it is that many of the changes which the Italians consider improvements are mere eye-sores, deformities, and sheer Vandalism in the estimation of foreign æsthetic tourists. The qualities that foreign visitors are apt still to admire among the Italians of the present day are their quick intelligence, their unfailing good humour, innate gentleness, courtesy and amiability, their unwearied readiness to oblige; but as a reverse of the picture, they find fault with the people's unconquerable idleness and frivolity, with their want of dignity and self-respect, their hot blood and bilious temperament; with their nature equally prone to give in to violent passions, and apt to dissemble them, to brood over and nurse them till a chance offers for their gratification.

In other words (the words of old geography class-books for English school-children): "The Italians are a dark but handsome race, clever, polite, and lively, great in music and painting, but (I quote from memory) hot-tempered and fierce, lazy and false, fond of pleasure, pomp, and ceremony, jealous, lascivious, vindictive, and superstitious."

The portraiture is altogether not flattering, but

may perhaps be admitted as true in the main, both on its bright and on its shady side. After all, I believe, no man ever dived more deeply into the idiosyncracies of the Italian character than Shakespeare, a man who probably never saw Italy, but who took the Italians at their own valuation, relying for his creations on the patterns supplied by the crude but naïve narrative of those *Novellieri*, or story-tellers, on which the plot of most of his plays was grounded. Such thorough gentlemen, such free-handed loyal friends, as Antonio, Bassanio, Lorenzo; such clever, lively, loving women as Portia and her maid Nerissa, might be found as easy in the Venice of our day as in that of Shylock; nor would it be difficult to fall in with such instances of blind, savage jealousy as Othello's, or of such subtle cunning and thorough-paced villainy as Iago's. Shakespeare painted men, and well knew how like human nature was in all countries; but he chose his subject among southern men, where he thought, with good reason, that the milk of that ubiquitous human nature was so peculiarly affected by the climate, as to flow freely and copiously from the heart in normal times, but also to turn terribly sour upon provocation; and as things were in Shakespeare's times, so they may be found, upon fair inquiry, at the present day.

In justice to the Italians, I shall make free to assert, that, as southern men, with kindred blood and analogous historical vicissitudes, under nearly the same climate, they are, to say the least of them, a little less cunning and treacherous than the Greeks; and with the same religion, somewhat less bigoted and truculent than the Spaniards. I could not claim less; in the worst of times generous men were willing to allow that "the Italians were not so black as they were painted"; and Byron, who lived long among them, declared in his sober moments that "they were better than their reputation." Allowing, therefore, that the moral standard of the nation had not during the period between Shakespeare and Byron fallen much lower than it was in the 'Merchant of Venice,' it would be worth while to inquire whether, from Byron's days to the present time, that same standard has risen any higher than it was in 'Beppo' or 'Don Juan.'

And, in the first place, without repeating what I have said with respect to the fitness of the Italians for military service, and the fact that, though not *born*, they may be *made* very good soldiers, I shall

take the liberty to deny that they are at all deficient
in that first and foremost requisite of manhood which
is called courage. An Italian, it is true, is not so
lavish of his life, not so ready and willing to break
his neck for mere sport, as those *amateur* steeplechase
jockeys and Alpine climbers, natives of a region "all
away from the sun's path," where, as Petrarch says,[1]
"a race of men is born for whom Death has no
pang." The horror of dissolution felt and abjectly
avowed by Claudio in 'Measure for Measure' (a
thoroughly Italian play, though the scene is laid
in Vienna), is only too natural in a country where
heaven and earth, day and night combine to invest
mere existence with inexpressible charm, and where
a gloomy religion has peopled with unspeakable
terrors the blank of the shadowy world beyond it.
But if Claudio is a genuine Italian, perfectly Italian
is also the heroine, his sister Isabella, the stern,
chiding monitress, when she urges that a thousand

[1] "Una parte del mondo è che si giace
    Mai sempre in ghiaccio ed in gelate nevi,
    Tutta lontana dal cammin del sole ;
    Là, sotto i giorni nubilosi e brevi,
    Nemica naturalmente di pace,
    Nasce una gente a cui'l morir non duole."
        Petrarch, Canzone II., 'A Iacopo della Colonna,
          esortandolo a favorir la Crociata,' stanza iv.

times more loathsome and hateful than death would be a shamed life.[1]

There we have the light and shade of the national character. Italian timidity, such as it is, has nothing in common with cowardice. Byron has said of that people that theirs was the true bravery, inasmuch as it springs from anger. Their organization may be more sensitive, their nerves less firmly strung; but rouse their passions, appeal to their feelings, and when "their blood is up," their wild-cat instincts will bear them up as efficiently as the French their dreams of glory, the Germans their drill and discipline, the Swiss their hope of good pay, and all nations indiscriminately what is called their "Dutch courage."

Alas! centuries have passed over Italy, during which all Church and State institutions conspired to make the nation a herd of cravens, to discountenance every exhibition of manly spirit. Foreign rulers dreaded nothing so much as the high spirit of their people. There could be for them no worse policy than to trust the natives with arms, to teach them the use of them, to organize them even as a civil guard,

---

[1] " *Isabella.* What says my brother?
Claudio. Death is a fearful thing.
Isabella. And shamed life a hateful."
           Shakespeare, 'Measure for Measure,' Act III. sc. i.

even as a fire brigade. To volunteer for police duty in great emergencies ; to lend a hand to the public force when worsted and nearly overpowered ; to step in even so far as to attempt to part the combatants in a street brawl, or to lift up the wounded from the pavement at the end of the fray,—all this was almost sure to bring a peace-loving or humane subject into serious trouble. *Rumores fuge* was the prescribed rule of conduct. On the slightest approach to disturbance, to tarry in the streets exposed the most inoffensive spectator or passer-by to be shot down like a dog. Everything was contrived to convince the citizen of his unfitness for all manly employment, and to make him rejoice in his exemption from all public service. In the Papal states, in the two Sicilies, where Swiss hirelings did the cut-throat business, it was the fashion to heap contempt upon the native troops, a Pope or a Bourbon being the first to speak words of disparagement about " Papal soldiers, of whom it takes ten to root up a turnip," or " Neapolitan soldiers, sure to run, however you may clothe them, and only fit to wear a breast-plate at their back, *that* being the only part they ever showed to an enemy."[1]

[1] " *Soldati del Papa, ce ne vuol dieci a cavar una rapa* " was the

At Rome and Naples, a priest in his dotage or
a craven prince made a dastardly army; but in
Piedmont, Victor Amadeus, himself a brave man,
was confident that "he had only to stamp with his
foot, and the soil of his country would yield him
as many soldiers as he had subjects."[1]   And it was
with those soldiers that himself and his successors
were able to hold their ground with honour, often
single-handed, against powers of the first rank.

As with the military, so about the civil courage
of the Italians.   Like latent fire, it requires nursing,
fanning, and rousing from the embers.   Certainly
nothing could be conceived more disgraceful than
the *sauve qui peut!* that rose in some of the Italian
cities, and especially in Naples, on the first outbreak
of the cholera.   Yet the good King Humbert had
only by his example to shame his subjects into a
decent behaviour, and forthwith a revulsion of feeling brought back the terrified fugitives to a sense
of their duty.   High and low, doctors, priests, men
and women, vied with one another in the cause of
humanity, with a zeal and heroism which was as

---

popular saying in Rome, and "*Fuiranno sempre*" in Naples, the
Sovereign who fed them giving the word.

[1] *Quanti sudditi, tanti soldati.*

steady and enduring as their panic had been sudden
and unreasonable. And the recovery at Palermo, in
the same straits, was so complete that the people,
upon hearing of the king's intention to come to their
aid, sent word that "they felt strong enough to
grapple with the dire epidemic without extraneous
succour," and besought His Majesty to put off the
honour of his intended visit to a more auspicious
opportunity, when he would be spared the heart-
rending sight of their affliction, and might join them
in their thanksgiving for their deliverance. In the
matter of Royalty, Italy obeyed the laws of natural
selection, and the survival of the fittest, which
equally applies to all things in nature. She cut
off the withered branches of Bourbon and Lorraine,
to make room for the growth and expansion of that
Savoy stem which had in it all the elements of a
robust and generous vitality. She set up a model of
princes which Germany and Spain, and more lately
Servia and Bulgaria, have been fain or forced to
imitate. Princes, who in all contingencies, be it of
war or peace, of health or illness, of flood or fire, of
conspiracy or rebellion, must always deem themselves
bound to take the lead, to *payer de leur personne.*

Akin to want of courage, and attendant upon it

like its shadow, is that other blemish in the national character which is commonly imputed to the Italians— want of truth. " All men are liars," said the Psalmist, " in his haste," and there were certainly reasons why the people of Italy should be no exception to the general rule. For in the clash of rivalries and hostilities of the European nations they had again and again to succumb to vastly superior numbers, and against the argument of brute force they had no other defence than craft. Both laws and creeds were imposed upon them at the sword's point. It was Jesuitism that taught them that all that was required of a man in the matter of religion was not *faith*, but *profession;* not *belief,* but *pretence.* What under princely and priestly tyranny was necessity of self-preservation, became matter of inveterate habit, and a wanton abuse of inventive powers. The lower classes in Italy, as in Ireland, in great measure learn to lie for the mere love of romancing. And the Neapolitans are never less to be believed than when they wind up their statements with the favourite phrase—" It is the truth I am telling you " (" *Non vi dico bugia*").

Strange to say ! Although the Italians are described as men of strong impulses, with quick feelings,

expressive features, and an amazing volubility of
tongue, they are at the same time credited with
great powers of dissimulation; they are said to be
fond of crooked ways, addicted to equivocation and
subterfuge, and acting upon the maxim that "language was given to man to conceal or disguise
thought." "The Italians," it is urged in one word,
"are the countrymen of Macchiavello."

And it is true: the Italians were in former times
a wide-awake people. They prided themselves in
that cleverness which borders on cunning. But cunning itself is merely a weapon in which there is no
harm so long as it is only used for defensive purposes.
The Italians were foremost in the race of European
nations; they excelled especially in the arts of
peace; they sketched the first rudiments of policy
and diplomacy. Papal Rome and Venice were the
first to send out ambassadors, "to lie for the good
of their country." There was something exceedingly
crooked, outrageous, diabolical in the political school
to which Macchiavello gave his name. But it could
scarcely be called Italian; it was simply human.
The Renaissance was Greek, Byzantine; there was
nothing more heathenish than the Christianity of the
Borgia and Medici Popes. But what was the religion

of Louis XI. of France, or Henry VII. of England? Machiavellism was the *thing* in Europe; Macchiavello only gave the *word*. No nation in Macchiavello's days was dealt by with greater treachery than poor Italy. Even Ludovico Sforza (or Ludovic the Moor) was hardly as false as the "honest Swiss" who sold him. Political contamination may have begun in Italy, but it did not stop there; if the Italians were the masters, they found everywhere wonderfully apt pupils, by the side of whom Macchiavello and his Florentine contemporaries were mere bunglers.

The Italians did not love war; but their *Condottieri* dignified strategy into a science and art, which gave mind its due preponderance over body. That everything was fair in war became an established principle. And the same latitude was soon allowed in politics and diplomacy, in love, in trade, in all private as well as public life. Success hallowed any stratagem by which any purpose might be accomplished.

And in all these matters, who will say that the Italians now-a-days are the masters of prevarication and subterfuge? or that it is to Italy that the epithet of "perfidious" is most generally or more justly applied? or that her diplomatists, her stock-brokers, her men of business, can hold a candle to the most innocent among their neighbours? It is not many years since Lord Chesterfield directed his son on his travels to court the acquaintance of the Piedmontese diplomatists, as "the most refined and accomplished gentlemen anywhere to be found." He did not say the "ablest men of business"; for Macchiavello's mantle had then already fallen to that school which produced the Talleyrands and Metternichs of latter days; and it is as much as the Sardinian envoys could then, or their Italian successors can now, do to stand their ground in a Paris or Vienna, a Berlin or Constantinople conference.

Cavour was the last statesman to give evidence of Italian subtlety and dexterity. He did not perhaps stick as strictly to a straight and open line of conduct as a disciple of the Bismarck "Blood and Iron" doctrine would approve; but the Italian Minister had not, like the German Chancellor, half a million bayonets at his back, always ready to give weight to his arguments. It was only by a great deal of shuffling the cards that poor Cavour could and did actually win the odd trick.

In private life, most assuredly, nothing is more peculiarly characteristic of the Italians than their utter want of reticence. They are as communicative, though not as inquisitive, as the Americans. One can hardly travel with any fellow passenger for half an hour in an Italian railway train without learning every particular concerning, not only himself, but also his wife, his mother, grandmother, and even mother-in-law. That under so many words there may lurk many lies is likely enough; but they must be at the utmost idle, clumsy, gratuitous lies. A shallow brawling brook will sooner show the pebbles at its bottom than a deep quiet pool. Were it even proved that of all men an Italian is the one that tells most lies, it is also certain that he is the one whose lies would soonest be found out.

Upon the same ground, we should hesitate to admit that the Italians are a bloody-minded people. They are eminently sociable, consequently they cannot afford to be very quarrelsome; they must show not a little mutual amiability and forbearance. Like all other southern men, they are irritable and vindictive. They are not such expert pugilists as the English, nor such eager duellists as the French; but they are apt to make too free with their knives, and not always in the mere blind heat of passion. They are loath to submit to insult, and must avenge it, regard-

less of the superior strength or skill that may stand
in the way of their resentment. They may be ready
to give life for life; but they must make sure of the
offender's life to begin with. It is the feeling which
animated the Highlander in Walter Scott's story of
'The Two Drovers.' By giving life for life a
murderer flatters himself he has paid his debt to
men's justice. The knife or the revolver, in the
opinion of the lower classes in Italy, is the only fair
means of neutralizing the advantage of bone and
muscle, on which an overbearing bully is tempted to
presume.

Sad that it should be so! There is something
appalling in the statistics of crime published yearly
in the Italian kingdom. And no doubt deeds of
blood swell the list in awful proportions; but far
more than to the resentful disposition of the people
the blame should in this matter be laid on the weakness and infatuation of their rulers. The Italians
are men of sudden, violent instincts. Their passions
should be, if not strongly, at least firmly curbed.
The punishment, if not adequate to the offence,
should at all events be prompt and unfailing. Unfortunately, the silly notions of a mawkish *humani-
tarianism*, the unconscionable dilatoriness of criminal

proceedings, the remissness, and in some cases venality of the police, and the insecurity of the prisons, are among the crying evils which conspired in the old despotic States, especially in Tuscany, Rome, and Naples, to foster in the worst criminals the hope of eventual impunity. And such disorders are still awaiting efficient remedies at the hand of the present national Government. With the rest of the world Italy should recover from the fatal epidemic of pseudo-philanthropy. In Italy, as elsewhere, and perhaps sooner than anywhere else, men should perceive how much easier it is to dismiss the hangman than permanently to dispense with his services. How improvident it is to spare the rod to spoil irreclaimable ruffians, to build up penitentiary palaces, to keep in clover and pamper incorrigible wild beasts in human shape. Like the rest of the world, like some of the Swiss cantons or Scandinavian kingdoms (which abolish their laws of Capital Punishment in December only to re-enact them in January), Italy will have to say, " *Que Messieurs les Assassins commencent les premiers.*" No one should have for thieves and murderers greater consideration than these worthies show to law-abiding and inoffensive subjects.

Italy must recover from the delusion prevailing all over the country, and especially in Tuscany, that mildness of punishment is the most efficacious deterrent of crime. She must begin to feel ashamed of the inconsistency with which, after nearly tearing from the hands of the police and lynching on the spot, a murderer taken red-handed, her people will, on the day of his trial, look upon the same monster as a *poverino*, a " poor victim," entitled to all their active sympathies. She ought to be shocked at the levity, the callousness, the cynicism with which murderers' escapes and murderers' acquittals are, owing to their frequency, dismissed from men's minds as mere trifles, slurred over with a short paragraph, or even a flippant joke, in the newspaper chronicle of current events.

" Four of the most atrocious criminals," we are told one day, " have broken from the Central Prison in Rome. There is great consternation in the neighbourhood. The police are on the ruffians' tracks." A few days later, in the same paper, perhaps, we read : " There are no tidings yet of the four desperate characters whose escape from prison was mentioned last week." And there, almost invariably, ends all further allusion to the subject.

And again : " Some labourers were at work near
Porta San Pancrazio. One of them, in sheer horse-
play, flung a small pebble at one of his friends which
hit him in the cheek ; forthwith he was requited by a
heavy slap, whereupon the two closed in deadly
scuffle : one fell to the ground stabbed to the heart,
the other broke through the midst of the horror-
stricken spectators, and was soon out of sight in the
open country."

This is all that is said, all that may ever be heard
of what is in Italy only too frequent and common-
place an occurrence. A life, a useful man's life, is
taken without rancour, upon the slightest provocation ; another man's life is possibly a prey to un-
ending regret and remorse for a deed, too evidently,
yet too irreparably, transcending the intention ; and
all in a brawl which in England would have had no
worse consequences than a " black eye," or a few
harmless bruises. It seems to strike no one wit-
nessing that vulgar tragedy, no one reading its
laconic report in the papers, that these are evils in
which prevention is better than cure. No one seems
to inquire, for instance, whether the practice of
carrying knives, revolvers, and other *armi insidiose*
(treacherous weapons) might not be put down by smart

penalties, though this was bravely and successfully accomplished at Genoa, when that city came into the possession of the Sardinian Government in 1815.

In the same manner, no one seems to inquire whether jailers, gendarmes, and all agents of the public force, could not, and should not, by the most stringent measures, be held strictly and inexorably responsible for the safe-keeping of the miscreants committed to their charge, even to the extent of making them amenable to the term of penal servitude in the prisons from which, owing to gross negligence or corruption on their part, the jail-birds have been let loose upon the world. And, also, whether the Court or the Home Office should not be amply and freely vested with the power of rescinding and annulling the absurd and wicked verdicts of *philanthropic* juries, by which the ends of justice are defeated, and the public consciences shocked and outraged to hear of "extenuating circumstances," or "irresistible force," pleaded in behalf of savage crimes of the most aggravated character.

I shall go further, and declare, that in the case of those *Ricatti*, or ransoms exacted by brigands for the release of the captives who have the ill-luck to fall into their hands, the Government, either by directing its own agents, or allowing the prisoner's friends to parley with the outlaws, and come to terms with them, paying the ransom, makes itself a partaker of the crime, an aider and abettor of the criminals.

No doubt, to cut off all communication, and abandon the kidnapped persons to the fate that may await them in the baffled ruffians' hands, would seem unheard of, cold-blooded cruelty; but no doubt, also, the practice of kidnapping would at once come to an end the moment the ruffians were taught by constant experience that the ransom would never have a chance of reaching them, and that their crime would thus, under no imaginable combination of circumstances, turn out profitable to its perpetrators. The captives would perish, most probably; but it is often " necessary that one man should suffer for the safety of a whole people." State surgery cannot hesitate about the amputation of a doomed limb, if it can thereby prevent the mortification of the others. Anything is better than the Government's direct or indirect compounding with evil-doers. Though more unfrequent on the mainland of Italy, these *Ricatti* are still occasionally heard of in some parts of Sicily; and while such is the case, Italy is still in this respect on a level of civilization with Greece and Turkey.

But apart from their proneness to give in to their wild passions, even under slight provocation, the generality of Italians cannot be taxed with deficiency of good nature towards their fellow beings; nor are they as wilfully cruel in their treatment of the brute creation as the "Humane Societies" would make us believe. The Italians, as a rule, are fond of their domestic pets even to silliness. If a Roman carter or a Neapolitan muleteer starves, over-loads, and over-drives his beast, if he belabours it within an inch of its life, it is simply owing to his poverty, to his want of temper, above all things, to his gross ignorance. "Why?—an animal," he has been taught by his priest, "is not a Christian; it has not a soul, it has no sense, no feeling; it is mere flesh and bone, mere stock and stone." In these matters the lower classes in Italy know no better than the brutes themselves. It is the law that is at fault; and things are not much better in other countries, where, in spite of an ubiquitous and vigilant police and heavy penalties, not only horses and asses, but even wives and children are often exposed to the most brutal treatment. With provident laws and their rigid observance, the Italians, as an intelligent and sober people, could be made as humane as their neighbours.

There are, unfortunately, other failings in Italy that the laws cannot reach. There are strong tendencies and propensities indifferently leading to good or evil, according as they are blindly indulged in and encouraged, or wisely controlled and directed. The Italians are not an intemperate race, but they are incontinent. And they are as ready to blame their hot climate for their weakness, as the English are to excuse their excessive fondness for strong drink on the plea of their damp and gloomy atmosphere.

I have already expressed my opinion that sensuality, the really besetting sin of the Italians, might and should be combatted in early life, and almost in infancy, by strong physical exercise and sound manly discipline. Give full scope to the bone and muscle, and you will leave less chance for the undue development of the nerve. And in the same manner, as a constant activity of the body is good for the child, so incessant occupation of the mind is recommendable to the grown-up man. Let life be like a stream of running water, leaving as little of it as possible to diverge into sluggish canals or stagnant pools.

The root of all mischief in old Italy was idleness and frivolity. It was not among the hard-worked and half-starved peasantry that vice could cast deep roots. It was in the upper middle classes, where, in the absence of all good stimulants to action, men looked for excitement in the gratification of passion —passion often as silly and frivolous as it was un-hallowed and degrading. The Italians for the most part are men of limited wants, tastes, and habits. No one can believe how cruelly most of them will stint and pinch themselves rather than work, reducing their expenditure and living upon next to nothing : breakfast at a *café*, dinner at a cheap *restaurant*, and a ticket for the opera make up all the necessaries and luxuries of life ; and all such commodities are, or were till lately, reduced to what in England would be considered fabulously low prices. But the first condition of this free-and-easy existence was that a man should have no one to provide for or think of besides himself. For the immense majority of loose men about town, the first of all luxuries to be re-nounced was that of a domestic establishment and of the most sacred affections. Nowhere in the world was celibacy more generally the order of the day than among the Italian middle classes. It was a law and sacrament for the whole brotherhood of priests and monks; a rule of discipline for the land and sea forces; absolute for the men, enforced by hard conditions upon the officers; a necessity for the mob of minor public functionaries and professional men; finally, a matter of fashion for the golden youth, to whose natural and lawful inclinations poverty could not be pleaded as a hindrance.

It would be superfluous to dwell on the complications of social disorders to which this abnormal condition of intersexual relations must needs give rise, especially in a country where passions, owing to a variety of causes, were allowed to run riot, and where men were over-fond of a vain display of morbid feelings and of exaggerated, if not affected sentimentalism. Where so many of the idlers about town were debarred from marriage, no wonder if some went about like lions seeking whom they might devour; in other words, considering "whose wife they should take." Owing to the *res angustæ domi*, and to the want of faith in his power to keep the gaunt wolf from the door by his good manly exertions, too poor to keep a wife, too lazy to work for a wife, an Italian, if he married at all, only did it late in life, and was seldom guilty of a pure love match. He turned out at the best an indifferent husband, and could look for little happiness from a wife whose inclinations had been, if at all, but slightly consulted.

There was very little mutual trust between a married couple in Italy. Affection was apt to die off, though jealousy not unfrequently survived. Bachelor's experience was not calculated to inspire a husband with faith in woman's virtue; too secluded an education in a nunnery, or at her mother's apron-strings, sent a bride to her wedded home unaware of her danger, unconscious of her duty, and as liable to fall from deficiency, as from excess of self-reliance.

Somehow, though instances of mutual esteem and lasting attachment between man and wife were by no means rare in Italy, it must be confessed that in the upper and middle classes domestic concerns were "all in the wrong." From the very dawn of intellectual life, from Dante and his Beatrice, from Petrarch and his Laura, down to Alfieri and his Royal Countess, men of genius in Italy seem to have laboured both by precept and example to dissociate love from marriage. A wedded life was apt to become as irksome as that of a couple of caged birds; it was looked upon, at the best, as a humdrum bondage, unsuited to persons with any pretension to the highest gifts of intellectual character. For all but the most common-place mortals, the Italians seemed to think love could be nothing but a burden the moment it became a duty.

This was a deplorable state of things, no doubt, an inveterate evil in that country, and which does not yet give all desirable signs of abatement among the living generation, though the consciousness of the dignity accruing to the country from its new political existence, a heartfelt and general wish for the rehabilitation of the national character, and also the necessity of meeting increased wants by redoubled exertions, unquestionably contribute to give society greater earnestness and manliness of tone, greater dignity and decency of behaviour. The Italians have not yet done much, they have not done enough, but seem now more bent on doing something towards "turning over a new leaf." They have less time, and can less afford to be dissipated or profligate.

Vice still exists in Italy, as elsewhere; but it obtrudes itself somewhat less under the old mask of

Platonism, or under the frivolous practices of *Cicisbeism*. There is already something gained by having things called by their own names. It should be borne in mind, also, that in these matters, though there must be fire, it is not probably at all proportionate to the intolerable deal of smoke that blinds men's eyes. There is a vast amount of exaggeration in the estimate of social disorder—an exaggeration which has its sources in the love of vile gossip and arrant scandal, natural to the vitiated habits of an idle people. In the frivolousness of their petty communities of former times, the Italians took an especial delight in painting themselves blacker than they were. Byron, I repeat, was sure that they improved on closer acquaintance, and it may be said of them, as of him, that they were in a great measure " *les fanfarons des vices qu'ils n'avaient pas.*"

Woman in Italy had at no time the honours she is entitled to. Feudalism never cast deep roots in the country, and many of the chivalrous feelings which that institution left behind in the Roman and Christian world never attained full development south of the Alps. Men in Italy make light in words of what, in fact, they value above all things, female virtue; for love with them is made up of

harassing jealousy and outrageous suspicion to an
extent unknown in other countries. From Boccaccio
to Ariosto and downwards, all Italian literature is an
endless variation on the trite theme : "Frailty, thy
name is woman." It is the subject of all after-dinner
talk, the topic of the foul-mouthed entertainment of
the idlers of the *cafés* in the towns, and of the
spezierie, or chemist-shops in the more primitive
villages. The Italians must recover from their un-
generous scepticism about woman's honour. It is
perhaps the very worst feature in their national character ; in that respect an Italian is hardly less at
the antipodes with an Englishman of our own day
than was the low-minded Roman Iachimo in Shakespeare's 'Cymbeline,' as contrasted with the loyal
and true-hearted Briton, Leonatus Posthumus. The
Italians should learn that it is confidence that begets
fidelity, that mistrust almost justifies, as it too often
provokes, simulation and treachery. How can a
woman be expected to be good if she is told that
all other women are "no better than they should
be." Women, like men, are apt to be led by example ;
they follow the fashion. Why should any wife aspire
to be an exception to the universal rule ? A phœnix !
that is not merely a rare but a *fabulous* bird !

In most other relations of life, Italian morality would better bear comparison with that of other nations. Domestic affections are not less strong in the south, though men there live more in the open air. Parental tenderness is often carried to the extremes of doting fondness; filial duties are frequently observed with little regard to manly self-reliance. Full-grown and almost grey-bearded men are seen tied, like mere babies, to their mothers' apron-strings ; submissive wives are by pusillanimous husbands exposed to the tyrannical caprices of a termagant mother-in-law. A clannish, gregarious feeling, common practice, or niggardly views of economy, not unfrequently keep together large families with several branches, and for two or more generations, under the same large palatial roof; a patriarchal promiscuousness, which in Italy is not in all cases unattended with a variety of discomforts, and even with some ill-smothered jarrings and bickerings ; but for which in England it would hardly be possible to devise any endurable *modus vivendi*.

There is no lack of rogues in Italy, of course, but nowhere can one find more honest and faithful domestic servants, especially where they are trusted and well-treated. Owing to the *mezzadria*, or half-profit system of husbandry, one half of the population, the townspeople, must needs leave their substance, the produce of their landed property, in a great measure at the discretion of the other half, receiving its rent in kind from the peasantry, an arrangement which implies no little uprightness on the part of the latter class, in spite of the familiar pun by which the landlord half-jocularly describes his *mezzadro* as *mezzo-ladro* (half thief), for that is what the peasant has it in his power to be when he chooses, and what he is all the more likely to become the more he is suspected and watched.

The time in which a school for petty thieves, especially from the person, flourished in Naples is perhaps not yet all over. But credit for superior skill and daring is now given by the Parisian to the "English pick-pockets," who are described as ubiquitous, and this may be applied to all sorts and conditions of thieves; for although there is still an immense number of rascals in Italy, it must be allowed that, in theft as in trade, the Italians are merely fit to carry on business on a small scale. Such wholesale financial plunderers as hover about the Stock Exchanges of great European and American commercial centres are comparatively unknown in

Italy; for grand operations in that country in State loans, railways, mines, canals, etc., are for the most part in the hands of "foreign industrials." Thieves south of the Alps are not yet all hanged; but there are few of them big enough to be knighted and ennobled, or admitted into the higher or lower Legislative Chamber.

CHAPTER IX.

CONCLUSION.

Recapitulation—Influence of New Institutions on the Old National Character—French Influence—Invasion of French Democracy —Symptoms of Reaction — The late Political Crisis — The Italian Parliament of the Future—Italy must Live and Learn —The Prospects of the Country as seen from various points of view—Conclusion.

I AM now at the end of my task. How have I acquitted myself of it? Let us sum up.

My object was to test the solidity attained within these last five-and-twenty years by the new edifice of Italian nationality.

Nations, we are told, are the makers of their own destinies. They give themselves the Government best suited to their natural disposition. Their rulers are the men of the people's own choice.

These truisms, however, have only lately been applicable to Italy. Five centuries of foreign mis-rule, imposed by irresistible force, had sunk the

Italians to the lowest depths of social and moral degradation, for which they could hardly be held responsible, and from which five lustres of independent existence could hardly have enabled them to recover, entirely and at once.

There is undoubted improvement, visible progress, material well-being, social movement, intellectual development in Italy. The only question is, whether the advance has been as rapid and steady as the Italians themselves imagined, and as their friends and enemies hoped or feared; whether the results of national emancipation have been for Italy all that the world looked forward to.

And, in the first place, whether what the Italians achieved was true independence, real self-government, whether they have had hitherto, or ever intend to have, a policy, a rule, a system of their own. Up to this time their institutions, their forms, their ideas were almost invariably borrowed from their neighbours, and certainly not from the best of them. Up to this time they have acted as if there were no country from which better notions could be imported than those which France for nearly a century has been spreading like a pestilence all over the civilized world : the false notions of liberty and equality, of

fraternity and humanity, of manhood suffrage and
popular sovereignty. And the truth is, Italy might
have wished for nothing better than that there should
have been a Chinese wall to shut out France and
whatever came from that quarter.

The Italians might have done better by consulting
their own past. No State was ever more completely
Frenchified than was old Piedmont towards the close
of the eighteenth century. But it happened that
Victor Amadeus III., a sovereign whose only thought
was his army, was smitten with a mad admiration for
the genius of Frederic II. of Prussia ; and, swayed
by this fancy, he gave not only to his army, but to
the whole organization of the State a German form
and colour. Who knows how much of the order and
discipline by which the Piedmontese soldiers and
statesmen took the lead in the work of national
emancipation, may be traceable to the traditions of
the narrow but sound martinet rule which that pig-
tailed and *tant-soit-peu* pig-headed king brought in
from the banks of the Spree ?

If the Italians must needs go to school abroad,
why should they not learn as much from the countrymen of Bismarck and Moltke, as from those of Thiers
and Gambetta, of Freycinet and Floquet ? Why

should they not look to German drill and discipline as the best antidote to French anarchic liberty?

It was from France that democracy found its way across the Alps. It was from France that came that blind faith in universal suffrage, in the infallibility of the masses, in the ever-sound instincts of a mere numerical majority, which has, if not disorganized the Italians, at least stood in the way of their re-organization. It is from France that the infatuation about the advantages of a Republic as the *grand ideal*, the model State, the only natural, perfect, and righteous form of civilized Government gained ground in a country which, even if it had not taken warning from the suicidal career of its own noblest mediæval free cities, might at least have profited by the three recent experiments of its Gallic neighbour, where Republicanism has proceeded from the tragedy of 1789, to the mere farce which awaits its *dénouement* in 1889.

In spite of the apostleship of Mazzini, I do not think that the Italians, as a people, are at heart democrats. The Italians are, as they undeniably ever were, good patriots : patriots, first, and then any-thing you please. Elsewhere love for the country was usually found blended with loyalty to the person

or the dynasty of a sovereign. In England, for
instance, a Charles Edward ; in France, a Chambord ;
in Spain, a Don Carlos, had it in their power to bring
upon the country all the disorders of a civil war.
But in Italy, who would ever draw a sword for a
Bourbon, an Este, or a Lorraine Pretender ? Who
would conspire for the restoration of a Pope-King ?
The Italians found only one of their reigning houses
wedded to the national cause, and hence the country
and that family were made one " for better, for
worse." When they most unjustly mistrusted Charles
Albert, they turned to Mazzini. But when Victor
Emmanuel led the way, nine out of ten of the
Mazzinians at once followed. In the same manner,
patriotism in Italy is stronger than Papism. Let
Leo XIII. be reconciled to Italy, and Italy will be
proud of her Catholicism. But the unity of the
country must be safe from religious as well as from
political dissension ; safe also from whatever remains
of mediæval municipalism. What one sees now-a-days
in Italy, is merely local egoism. There is no longer
a shadow of the rancours and jealousies of former
states ; but merely an instinct, only too natural,
though by no means laudable, in every town, province, or region, to look upon its own interests as

preponderant over the common good. What remains of municipalism is merely " Belfry Policy,"—a mean policy, which may lay a heavy charge on the Budget, but can involve no danger to the unity of the State. Even in hare-brained Naples or isolated Sicily the cry of " Home Rule" would never be raised. The phenomenon of a Gladstone would be an impossibility.

Clearly, with a little good management, the Italians have as little to fear from internal dissensions as from foreign complications. But self-government is a difficult art, and the Italians came to it with little previous experience, and under very trying material embarrassment. They did not, and could not, at first well regulate their expenses. They did not sufficiently provide for public security. They have not yet altogether rid the country of beggars or brigands. They did not give the national resources all the development of which they were susceptible. They broke down, sadly, in almost every branch of administration.

There is nothing surprising in all this, nothing to preclude the hope of better things. The Italians must live and learn, as other people have done before them. Only to make up for their short-comings, they must refer them to their causes. It is French democracy, French pedantry and self-sufficiency, that has done all the mischief in Italy, and something like a reaction is as desirable as it is unavoidable. The Italians are not blind to the terrible *Impasse* to which their French teachers have brought themselves. Whatever may become of France, Italy will undoubtedly have to retrace her steps. A nation which has a King Humbert at her head is not likely to fall under the dictatorship of a General Boulanger.

It is idle to suppose, as some do, that in politics there must be *vestigia nulla retrorsum*. It may be very hard, indeed, for a progressive nation to appear to stultify itself by acknowledging a mistake; but not when perseverance in a wrong course might prove fatal. It is never too late to mend. Not only what is ill-done *may*, but it not unfrequently *must* be undone. There can be no policy absolutely irrevocable, no principle irremovably established. If any matter, for instance, ever seemed inexorably settled in England, it was " Free Trade." " Discussion on the subject," it was said, " is thoroughly exhausted. Protection is to all eternity dead and buried, never to come to light again." But the answer is, " Not the *word*, perhaps, but what of the *thing ?* Not

'*Free Trade*,' by all means; but what of '*Fair Trade?*'"

The same reasoning may apply to French institutions as they have been imported into Italy. The cry of the Florentines when Guerrazzi with his *sbarazzini*, or *Roughs*, of Leghorn were kicked out in 1849 was, "*Vogliamo i Galant'uomini*" (our rulers must be honest men, or gentlemen); and the same cry was heard almost all over Italy during the recent general election of April (1886). And throughout the period of the new Italian era, in most of the communes, and especially in the large cities (in which the traditions of old Italian municipal institutions survived in the worst of times), in spite of the broadest popular suffrage, the choice of a Syndic, or Mayor, very generally falls on a conspicuous personage, usually a nobleman.

It is otherwise with Parliamentary elections: because the multitude, with whom the choice of candidates rests, vote more absolutely in the dark, care less about the result of the polls, and are more helplessly at the discretion of misleading stump-orators and of an unscrupulous half-penny Press. The Italians have not yet come to universal suffrage; but they are very near it, and they will soon find out (if indeed they have not by this time done so) that they have already been carried too far, and that it is time to fall back.

Up to the accomplishment of Italian nationality by the occupation of Rome, in 1870, merely political or social questions had hardly ever been mooted. The statesman of the Cavour school who led triumphant Italy to the gates of the Eternal city, had governed the country upon the principles of the Charles Albert *Statuto*, or Charter, with a Parliament elected on the somewhat narrow but reasonably liberal Electoral law of the same epoch.

Unfortunately, only a few years after the instalment of the Italian Government in its permanent capital, the disciples of the Cavour school lost their seats in the Cabinet, and a new administration was formed, March, 1876, the members of which belonged to the Left, or Radical party of Rattazzi.

Since that time Italy, in spite of frequent but short intervals, and slight and unimportant changes, has been for ten years (1876—1886) under the control of Depretis, the Lieutenant and successor of Rattazzi—a gloomy, ungenial, saturnine man, with a sour look and a sepulchral voice, who, without the activity or *chauvinistic* patriotism of a Thiers, or the muddled scholarship and clap-trap eloquence of a Gladstone, had enough of the senile ambition and low cunning of both to make himself as indispensable in Italy as the first of the two above-named ever was in France or the second in England.

For the whole of this period under Depretis, and the supporters or rivals whom he by turns took up and dropped as colleagues in his Cabinet, the work of demoralizing by democratizing the country proceeded at a rapid pace.

Italian politicians, be it observed, no matter what party they belonged to, have not, on the whole, been self-seeking. These men of the Left, bent on governing by the people, seemed to care little whether they acted for the people's benefit or to their detriment. Their aim was to place the two-edged weapon of manhood suffrage in the hands of the multitude, little heeding whether the multitude used it in self-defence or to its own destruction. Whatever the ministers wished, whatever they asked, the enormously enlarged franchise and the compact majority issuing from it in the Chamber unconditionally vouchsafed them. For, sure of the people's vote, Democracy drives a country to its ruin as infallibly as " A beggar mounted rides his horse to death."

Personal bribery is as yet almost unknown in Italy. Italian Ministers, to do them justice, seldom if ever take, Italian Deputies seldom if ever ask, anything for themselves. But for their electors, for their friends and supporters, for their village, town, or province, in one word, for their "Belfry," every man who has a vote, either at the poll or the Chamber, seems always ready to sell himself to the highest bidder. And certainly no Minister ever bid so high as Depretis, who seems to think, not as Walpole, that "every man has his price," but that every constituency is purchasable. With his electoral law of 1882, he indeed might flatter himself that he had bought up the Italian nation wholesale. He was the statesman who insured the support of the Senate or Upper House by the creation of as many as seventy new Senators at one batch. He it was who mustered up a majority in the Lower House by that "Monster Railway Bill" of 6000 miles, by which he sent back his gratified supporters to the polls, each member the bearer of the plan of some new trunk or branch line for his particular *College*, or electoral district—a boon to the locality which could not fail to insure the re-election of every Ministerial candidate—a bribe which scarcely anywhere failed to accomplish its purpose.

The policy of a Ministry granting every locality whatever it asks, whether it wants it or not, and even anticipating its wishes, cannot fail to be popular ; but its success must needs be ephemeral, for it is an expensive policy, and it involves a great increase of taxation ; and the results are, either that the taxes are made to weigh equally on the whole people, in which case they create general discontent, or they are laid upon certain classes for the benefit of certain others, when the consequence is an antagonism, not unlikely to lead to a war of classes. The system of the Depretis administration aimed at relieving the lower at the expense of the upper orders ; and, of course, for measures of that nature, the electoral law of 1882 was a tower of strength ; for by it the Ministry brought the overwhelming voice of the multitude to bear against the influence of the intelligence of the population, and thus enlisted on the side of the Government all the strength of what Carlyle called "the Lack-alls."

It was not long, however, before the whole country, including the sounder and more rational faction of the Left party, and its chief, Depretis himself, became aware that matters had been carried too far, that the democratization of the country had reached the limit beyond which a reaction had become unavoidable. Depretis, whose only object after attaining the supreme power was simply to retain it, seeing in what direction the tide was setting, took it at the turn, and by the aid of the men of the Right, or Conservatives, overcame his most rabid associates of the Extreme Left, in February 1886, and insured a working majority in his appeal to the country of the ensuing May.

This was a first step of Italy on her return to a moderate policy; but it was neither a thorough nor a decisive movement; for the Conservatives, who had on that occasion the casting vote, had, by the death of Sella and the ill-health of Minghetti,[1] been left without an acknowledged chief of their own, and by accepting the leadership of Depretis, they lost much of their dignity, without to any extent promoting the triumph of their principles.

Reaction had been attempted but not accomplished. The mischievous electoral law is still in force, and may still lead to that universal suffrage which has made a Boulanger possible in France, and the mere approach to which has so nearly placed the unity of the British Empire at the mercy of a Gladstone.

---

[1] Since dead. Dec. 1886.

In her progress towards democracy Italy has not been alone; she has been whirled along in a vortex which is threatening to involve all Europe in a common ruin, and into which it should have behoved a new and untried nation not to throw herself. There are questions, a great many vital questions, in which Italy is interested, but not more so than other nations. All that concerns popular sovereignty, popular education, and especially the great matter of the mutual relations between Church and State, has supplied for many years the themes of passionate debate in great and long established communities, which could best allow themselves costly innovations, and even dangerous experiments. England, for instance, could pass from protection to Free Trade, and from Free Trade to Fair Trade, and yet perhaps thrive by both changes. France might plunge into all the mad extremes of the Republic or the Commune, and still emerge from her present "slough of Despond" and live. But Italy has not for the present reached that degree of consistency, she is not yet sufficiently sure of herself to venture too far out of her depth. She should not presume to cut the intricate knots that all Europe is painfully labouring to untie.

By dealing with the main social problems which

interest all mankind, Italy's mighty neighbours are
doing her work as well as their own. Italy should
live and learn; she will have to follow for many
years ere she be in a position to take the lead. And
the worst perhaps is that she fancies she pursues her
own course, when she is only taken in tow by France.

What is at fault in Italy, as in many other
countries, is really discipline: it is the law, with its
absurd mildness and leniency, and the culpable remissness of its appointed executors. The Italians
were, in despotic times, wont to look upon the law
as the direct instrument in the hand of tyranny.
The hatred which prompted and almost justified its
open violation, or subtle evasion, degenerated into
contempt when the reign of King Log superseded
that of King Stork, *i. e.* when the Government, though
still absolute, became effete and idiotic, and the people
baffled the law, not any longer by defying, but simply
by wholly ignoring it. But how must it be now,
under a Parliamentary *régime* showing so much more
eagerness about the quantity than the quality of its
enactments?

In despotic times the motto was, " *Comandi chi
può, ubbidisca chi deve* " (Let every man do as he is
bid) ; but in constitutional times it has been changed

to " *Comandi chi può, ubbidisca chi vuole* " (Let every man do as he pleases). The word *Liberty* is defined as a man's right to do what he likes, evil as well as good; the word *Humanity* as impunity for evil-doers. The millennium of modern philanthropists is the abolition of the gallows for the most atrocious murderers, and of the lash for the most incorrigible ruffians.

At the time I was about to leave Italy, in the early days of May of this year, 1886, men's minds were painfully alive to the crisis which Depretis' dissolution of Parliament had compelled the country to go through. One Chamber was dismissed, and there seemed to be a chance of even a worse issuing from the electoral urns. It was expected to spring from lower social layers, and it requires all the faith of Mazzinianism to believe that " the lower you go, the sounder and purer you find the popular masses." These sinister forebodings, however, were not in this encounter borne out by the results. The Conservatives carried the day, not because they constituted a majority, but because Depretis' defection split the Left into two factions, the strongest of which followed its leader into his former enemies' camp. The victory of the party of order was, however, saddened by a few scandalous incidents; in two different constituencies, Ravenna and Forli, the votes of a large majority were given in behalf of one Cipriani, a man convicted of three murders, because the populace, not satisfied with the verdict of the jury and the sentence of the court, chose to look upon the prisoner as a martyr, and hoped to defeat the ends of justice by investing a mere criminal with the inviolable character of a national representative. In Rome itself, and in its very first district, Don Fabrizio Torlonia, a most liberal and popular patrician, as well as a thorough man of business, was worsted in a very stoutly contested election; the multitude being determined to force the Government's hand (as it eventually did) by freeing from well-deserved punishment a man named Coccapieller, formerly a Swiss soldier in the Papal Guard, but in latter years a naturalized Italian subject, a notorious demagogue and self-styled "Tribune," fitted by nature to be set up for a very idol of the lowest populace.

There was thus something cheering, but far from reassuring, in the upshot of the electoral experiment of last May. In the first place, although the battle was won on the Conservative side, this was mainly because the millions of voters who were so lately entrusted with the franchise by the new electoral law, did not yet feel their own strength, and only put it forth in some localities, as in the three above-named towns, under the influence of blind passion and perverted judgment; acting thus like the Jews when bidden to choose between Christ and Barabbas.

In the second place, because the new Chamber, which was at work only for a few days before the long summer recess, did not, even in the mere fag-end of a session, evince that self-respect and sense of duty, which might have justified the hope of its being an improvement upon those which preceded it.

The positive result of the great crisis of 1886 was merely to establish the unbounded ascendancy of Depretis.

And Depretis is still, as he has been for ten years, at the head of affairs, not so much because there was no one *able*, but because there was no one *willing*, to step into his place, to take up that *damnosa hereditas* of wholesale corrupt practices by which the old shuffler contrived to impose himself upon the country; because in the sorest hour of need a man was not forthcoming.

Depretis is far from being immortal. Indeed, he is not in good health; he looks worn-out and decrepit.

But to judge from the zeal both of his old friends and of his former adversaries, one would think that after him there can be nothing for Italy but the Deluge.

Strange to say, the country which five-and-twenty years ago, with the Austrians still in Venice and the French in Rome, mourned for, but managed to survive Cavour, seems now to find it impossible to get on without Depretis !

The real truth is, perhaps, that "there is something rotten in the State" of Italy. It may well be pedantry to remind the Italians that the real worth of a nation is but the sum of all its private and domestic virtues ; that a people deaf to the sense of duty is hardly entitled to exercise any right ; that a people who never learned to obey has done nothing to fit herself for command.

Who knows it not ? These are truisms easily established in theory ; but how many are there to carry them out into practice ? Since 1859 the population has largely increased in Italy ; more work is done, more wealth has been accumulated. But can we feel sure that this increase of material well-being in some classes is attended by a corresponding improvement of the conditions of all the other classes ?

Must it not, on the contrary, be evident, that the lower instincts—luxury, avarice, envy, and other deadly sins—have been all these years gaining the upper hand? Does it not too frequently happen that where you are looking for the country, you only find the town or province, the district or parish? that where you appeal to patriotism, you are only answered by egoism?

"Oh!" it may be retorted, "what would you have? The Italians are but men, neither more nor less, neither better nor worse than other men—as good as the French, the English, and Germans."

Perhaps so. Be it so. But Italy is not France, England, or Germany. Italy is a nation which needs strengthening, renewing, rehabilitating; which must regain the world's respect. Italy aspired to self-Government. What can be said worse about her than that she has fallen under the rule of an "Indispensable Man"?

To this condition Italy has been brought by five lustres of French democracy, by the maxim that, "one man is as good as another, and even perhaps a deal better;" by the notion that a free citizen has a right to *all* liberties, even to that of doing wrong; that laws are only made to be broken; and that in a free state, whoever may be appointed to command, no one is bound to obey.

In little more than five lustres Italy has brought herself to the condition of *"La France Acéphale"* (headless France). There is hardly a class, hardly a party, hardly a *clique*, large or small, hardly an individual, in a position to preside over the country's destinies. There is, it is true, a king—the best of kings. But then modern democracy will only tolerate a king who "reigns and rules not."

Italy has reached only half the goal aimed at by Mazzini when he wished to enthrone *"Dio e il Popolo"* (God and the people). The people is sovereign, but God is nowhere. What have the Democrats done with Him? They have broken the laws, the earthly ties of man to man, and they have trampled on religion, *i. e.* on conscience, which is the Divine link by which alone human bonds can be securely riveted.

"Away with the Pope! Down with the Priest! Up with Godless schools in a Godless State! Such is the democratic clamour in Italy; in that benighted country where nine-tenths of the living population can no more exist without their *Santa Messa* (Holy Mass) than without their daily bread; and the other tenth consists of arrant infidels, who dare not die

without crying, not God! God! but '*Un prete!
Un prete!*' For God's sake, send for a priest!"

Much is said about United Italy. But where is
the bond of union? Behold! two Italies: one a
believing, the other a sceptic Italy. Can we reconcile Church and State? Jesuitism and patriotism?
Even if, with Carlyle, we look upon the Pope as the
"Old Chimæra," can we hope to convert him, or to
depose him? It is very easy to say "*Les Dieux s'en
vont;*" but can we dispense with other gods? Mazzini had a full faith in a new religion, and he was
ready to take upon himself its apostleship. But
Mazzini's Gospel, like Saint Simonianism, only tended
to demolish social order, and what we want is to
reconstruct it.

To whom is the task of reconstruction to be
entrusted? There are in Italy men of high qualities
—lofty minds, noble hearts, righteous intentions,
austere virtues. But these are individual gifts, not
much known, and even less valued. No one looks
for the best man. The noisiest—the *Coccapiellers*—
carry everything before them. Democracy is every-
body's government; demagogy is the government
of the very worst.

With what hope or with what faith then is Italy

looking forward to her future? Where are the elements of her strength? where is the basis of her
greatness? On what material, intellectual, or moral
forces rests the certainty of her independence and
unity, of her very existence?

Out of the many persons entitled to my highest
esteem, from whom I took leave as I was departing
from Italy this last May (1886), there was not one
that gave me a word of comfort.

"In Italy," they said, "we are still, thank heaven!
a thousand miles away from the Republic. King
Humbert and all the Savoy Dynasty are too wise
and too loyal, too universally and deservedly popular
to allow us to fall into those excesses which have
made France a bye-word among civilized nations.
Still there is something, there is much that is foul
and unwholesome in Italy, and more perhaps than
may be curable by merely strict constitutional means.

"There is a weariness, an apathy, a *marasmus*, a
tendency even among the better classes to despair
of themselves, to withdraw from public affairs, and
declare that they will have nothing further to do
with politics, as if politics were a trade or profession,
like the stage, like law, or physic, from which one
could fall back as soon as a man's fortune is made,

or the hope of it renounced ; as if by throwing up his country's interests one did not endanger and damage his own ; as if by his retirement he did not risk making room for adventurers and busy-bodies, for rogues and fools, in whose hands private as well as public fortunes may come to irreparable grief; as if the example of France and Spain, and of other ultra-democratic communities on either side of the Atlantic, did not teach us that, if men make themselves sheep the wolves will devour them."

The situation, in the opinion of these estimable old friends and contemporaries of mine, was full of danger, and it called for the utmost exertions of all good men and true.

" It called especially," they said, " for the personal intervention of the ' good and true ' King Humbert, who, acting either by his own initiative and upon his sole responsibility, or at the suggestion of a trusty adviser, should resort to some decisive measure, to some solemn and generous appeal from the drunken to the sober nation."

" It was thus," Humbert should be reminded, " that his father, Victor Emmanuel, and his good angel, Massimo d'Azeglio, saved Piedmont from its own infatuation in 1849, when they made their refractory Chamber swallow a peace which was as necessary as it was (under all circumstances) most honourable : they did it by that Moncalieri Proclamation, which will be as great a landmark in the history of future Italy as the Hegira is in the annals of Islamism."

There were other persons, however, perhaps of a more truculent temperament, who seemed convinced that "the cure of their country's sores cannot be left to the mere salve or sticking-plaster of either king or minister; but must be the result of a firm surgical application of steel and fire; it must be effected by that more or less severe and long ordeal of adversity, of wars and revolutions, which Italy had, too fortunately, to a great extent escaped at the time of her emancipation, but which hangs upon her as an unpaid debt—that ordeal which alone will have power thoroughly to re-temper, to redeem and ennoble her national character, even as a thunder-storm clears and purifies the atmosphere."

But others, again, of a less gloomy disposition, seemed to see no necessity, either for violently re-actionary or for well-meant but arbitrary courses. "The evil exists," they acknowledged; "but it must be allowed to wax much greater before one may hope that it will cure itself. Leave must be given to blatant democracy to bawl itself hoarse, to wear itself out; for, however demoralizing its influence may have been in Italy, it will never have reached, and never will reach such extremes; it will never fall into such mad-dog excesses as men have witnessed in France. Somehow Italy has the knack of stopping on the brink of an abyss. There is a good deal of Celtic blood in that country; but it does not run so wild as on the western watershed of the Alps, or on the western coast, the wrong side of St. George's Channel. There might be no great conceit in saying that the Italians are wiser than the French or Irish."

" Italy," these my hopeful friends aver, " is, in the end, always sure to alight on her feet. No other force than reason is required in that country to obtain such modifications of existing institutions as may be deemed consistent with the fundamental liberties which the sacred compact between king and people has made inviolable. ' Anybody,' said Cavour, ' might govern with a state of siege.' But the Italians abhor a statesmanship *à la Bismarck;* they have gone so far without revolutions, they would fain proceed to the end without reaction."

Such, as far as I could make out, was the conflict

of opinions in Italy in the early summer of 1886. But the heat of the season in which no man can work brought about the wonted truce which could only end at the re-opening of the Chambers. As I am now laying down my pen, the time of the year for the re-awakening of political and social life is rapidly nearing. Italy will again take up the thread of her history. What destinies are in store for her, whether her sanguine or her gloomy prophets, her optimists or pessimists, have more accurately hit the mark, events will make clear even to those unused to read the future in the diligently consulted experiences of the past.

THE END.

R. Clay and Son, London and Bungay.

11, HENRIETTA STREET, COVENT GARDEN, W.C.

NOVEMBER, 1886.

A

Catalogue of Books

PUBLISHED BY

CHAPMAN & HALL,

LIMITED.

FOR

Drawing Examples, Diagrams, Models, Instruments, etc.,

ISSUED UNDER THE AUTHORITY OF

THE SCIENCE AND ART DEPARTMENT,
SOUTH KENSINGTON,

FOR THE USE OF SCHOOLS AND ART AND SCIENCE CLASSES,

See separate Illustrated Catalogue.

THOMAS CARLYLE'S WORKS.

Messrs. CHAPMAN & HALL are now publishing an entirely New Edition of the Writings of Mr. Carlyle, to be completed in Seventeen Volumes, demy 8vo, called

THE ASHBURTON EDITION.

This Edition is handsomely printed, contains all the Portraits and Illustrations, and is issued in Monthly Volumes, at Eight Shillings a Volume, viz. :

BOOKS

PUBLISHED BY

CHAPMAN & HALL, LIMITED.

ABLETT (T. R.)—

WRITTEN DESIGN. Oblong, sewed, 6d.

ABOUT (EDMOND)—

HANDBOOK OF SOCIAL ECONOMY; OR, THE
WORKER'S A B C. From the French. With a Biographical and Critical Introduction by W. FRASER RAE. Second Edition, revised. Crown 8vo, 4s.

AGRICULTURAL SCIENCE (LECTURES ON), AND
OTHER PROCEEDINGS OF THE INSTITUTE OF AGRICULTURE, SOUTH KENSINGTON, 1883-4. Crown 8vo, sewed, 2s.

THE ARMIES OF THE NATIVE STATES OF INDIA.
Reprinted from the *Times* by permission. Crown 8vo, 4s.

BADEN-POWELL (GEORGE)—

STATE AID AND STATE INTERFERENCE. Illustrated by Results in Commerce and Industry. Crown 8vo, 9s.

BARKER (G. F. RUSSELL) and DAUGLISH (M. G.), of Lincoln's Inn. Barristers-at-Law.

HISTORICAL AND POLITICAL HANDBOOK. Crown 8vo, 6s.

BARTLEY (G. C. T.)—

A HANDY BOOK FOR GUARDIANS OF THE POOR.
Crown 8vo, cloth, 3s.

BAYARD: HISTORY OF THE GOOD CHEVALIER,
SANS PEUR ET SANS REPROCHE. Compiled by the LOYAL SERVITEUR; translated into English from the French of Loredan Larchey. With over 200 Illustrations. Royal 8vo, 21s.

BELL (JAMES, Ph.D., &c.), Principal of the Somerset House Laboratory—

THE CHEMISTRY OF FOODS. With Microscopic
Illustrations.
PART I. TEA, COFFEE, COCOA, SUGAR, ETC. Large crown 8vo, 2s. 6d.
PART II. MILK, BUTTER, CHEESE, CEREALS, PREPARED STARCHES, ETC. Large crown 8vo, 3s.

BENNET (*WILLIAM*)—

KING OF THE PEAK: a Romance. With Portrait.
Crown 8vo, 6s.

BENSON (*W.*)—

MANUAL OF THE SCIENCE OF COLOUR. Coloured
Frontispiece and Illustrations. 12mo cloth, 2s. 6d.

PRINCIPLES OF THE SCIENCE OF COLOUR. Small
4to, cloth, 15s.

BINGHAM (*CAPT. THE HON. D.*)—

A SELECTION FROM THE LETTERS AND
DESPATCHES OF THE FIRST NAPOLEON. With Explanatory Notes.
3 vols. demy 8vo, £2 2s.

THE BASTILLE. 2 vols. Demy 8vo.
[In the Press.

BIRDWOOD (*SIR GEORGE C. M.*), C.S.I.—

THE INDUSTRIAL ARTS OF INDIA. With Map and
174 Illustrations. New Edition. Demy 8vo, 14s.

BLACKIE (*JOHN STUART*), F.R.S.E.—

THE SCOTTISH HIGHLANDERS AND THE LAND
LAWS. Demy 8vo, 9s.

ALTAVONA: FACT AND FICTION FROM MY LIFE
IN THE HIGHLANDS. Third Edition. Crown 8vo, 6s.

BLATHERWICK (*CHARLES*)—

PERSONAL RECOLLECTIONS OF PETER STONNOR,
Esq. With Illustrations by JAMES GUTHRIE and A. S. BOYD. Large crown 8vo, 6s.

BLOOMFIELD'S (BENJAMIN LORD), MEMOIR OF—
MISSION TO THE COURT OF BERNADOTTE. Edited by GEORGIANA,
BARONESS BLOOMFIELD, Author of "Reminiscences of Court and Diplomatic Life."
With Portraits. 2 Vols. demy 8vo, 28s.

BOYLE (*FREDERICK*)—

ON THE BORDERLAND—BETWIXT THE REALMS
OF FACT AND FANCY. Crown 8vo, 10s. 6d.

BOULGER (*DEMETRIUS C.*)—

GENERAL GORDON'S LETTERS FROM THE
CRIMEA, THE DANUBE, AND ARMENIA. 2nd Edition. Crown 8vo, 5s.